Different
from the Other Kids

A Book of Interviews for Parents of Challenging Children

ANGELA TSOUNIS

Copyright © Angela Tsounis 2015
Cover Design by HyperSuasion Consulting
Published by HyperSuasion Consulting Ltd, Ontario, Canada

First edition published October 2015
ISBN: 978-0-9937703-2-6 (Kindle edition)
ISBN: 978-0-9937703-9-5 (Print edition)
Printed in the US and Europe

All Rights Reserved. No part of this book may be reproduced or utilized in any form or by any means, electronic or mechanical, including photocopying, recording, or by any information storage and retrieval system, without written permission from the publisher.

Dedication

*For those kids who are difficult to figure out,
and their parents who make it their mission to do so.*

&

*For Muriel, who stood fast and strong in her support of
Christina's Mother and never let her feel alone.*

Acknowledgments

I would like to express my gratitude to the many people who saw me through this book.

To those that have contributed their considerable time and were gracious enough, and in some cases brave enough, to be interviewed and share your story, I give you heartfelt and loving thanks. Some have been acknowledged here with pseudonyms, some with full disclosure; but all gave unselfishly to our readers and listeners. You help give clarity and insight when so few will step-up and have their voice heard. I will be forever grateful.

I would like to thank my partner, Melinda, for the constant support, for her insistence that this project was important and for loving my kids and me so deeply. Thank you for your patience with my life: I think I did warn you that it's never boring!

I also want to thank my wonderful children. Thank you to Christina. You continue to amaze me with your love and resilience. You are inspiring. Through you I found strength I didn't know I had. Thank you to Zoe for always standing strong. You have always been our rock. Thank you for always giving us a hand to hold when things go off the rails. Thank you to Dimitri for always making me smile. Thank you for your sense of wonderment and integrity.

This book would not have been possible without the unflagging support and hard work of my nephew, Project Coordinator and Business Developer, Jesse Bickerton. Jesse has had input in every aspect of this project. Your help has been invaluable. Without you, this project might be forever unfinished. Jess, we did it!

Thank you to my brother, Michael, for helping us through an extremely difficult year. You single-handedly dealt with finalizing Mom's estate, allowing me to keep my head clear (many times through tears) to complete this project.

Thank you to my 'front line' editors, Jennifer Wales, Zoe Tsounis and Jesse Bickerton who not only collected mistakes, but helped make difficult conversational transcriptions make sense on the page.

I owe a huge thanks to Rob Cuesta of HyperSuasion Consulting. Thank you for being a real consultant. You provided great ideas, clarified all the steps necessary to make this effort 'go' and ensured the project got its best positioning on Amazon and iTunes. I thank you for the vision and some necessary 'polish'. You are a credit to the marketing profession.

Table of Contents

Introduction	1
A Note On Language	5
The Day I Found Out I Was Bipolar	7
Breaking-Up Is Hard To Do	23
Never A Victim, But Forever A Fighter	37
What I Gained From Losing Everything	51
Tough Love	63
Dealing With Intolerance And How I Got Through It	73
The Power Of Art	83
The Art Of Mental Illness	99
Getting Lost In The System Part I	115
Getting Lost In The System Part II	127
It Takes Two	141
A Team Approach	155
Don't Ignore Your Gut	163
Shame Is Only A Perception	173
Contributing And Staying Connected	181
A Quick Fix Is Just A Quick Fix	189
Conclusion	201
Listen to the Different From the Other Kids Podcast	209
Reader Resources	210

Disciaimer
The (Not So) Small Print

It's truly sad that we live in a world where I have to write this section, but my lawyer, my accountant and my publisher have all told me they will be <u>very unhappy indeed</u> if I don't put this in, and the last thing I want is an unhappy publisher on my back, so here it is.

I, Angela Tsounis, am not a doctor, and I certainly don't pretend to be one on paper. I am not even that well educated. I'm a parent. Period. The advice presented in *Different from the Other Kids* does not replace advice received directly from a medical health professional. If you think you need help, I do recommend making an appointment with your physician or other appropriate health care provider.

The author, the publisher and the parents and professionals interviewed for this work make no representations or warranties with respect to the accuracy or completeness of the contents of this work, including, and without limitation, warranties of fitness for a particular purpose.

The content, case studies and examples shared in this work should not be assumed to represent, in any way, medical or professional advice. Neither the author nor the publisher is familiar with you, your child or your circumstances. You alone are responsible for your actions and, and in your use of these materials, you agree not to hold us liable for any of your decisions, actions or results, at any time, or under any circumstances.

No portion of this work is intended to offer legal, medical, personal or financial advice. If professional assistance is required, the services of a competent professional should be sought. Neither the publisher nor the author shall be liable for damages arising herefrom.

Under no circumstances, including but not limited to negligence, will the author or publisher, or any of their representatives or contractors be held liable for any special or consequential damages that result from the use of, or inability to use, the materials, information, or strategies communicated through this work, or any services following this work, even if advised of the possibility of such damages.

The fact that an organisation, individual or website is referred to as a source of further information does not mean that the author or the publisher endorses the information the organisation or website may provide, or recommendations it may make. Further, readers should be aware that internet websites listed in this work may have changed or disappeared between when this work was written and when it was read.

In other words, nothing in this book should be taken as any form of contractual obligation. Neither the author, nor her publisher, nor the owners of the intellectual property rights to the book or their assignees warrant any result from acting upon the ideas in this book, and we accept no liability for any damage, loss or harm to you or any third party arising from any interpretation or implementation of the ideas in this book.

And with that out of the way...

Introduction

Christina's beautiful six year old face was contorting, like she was having some sort of strange spasm. She had constant facial grimaces. She was always clenching her jaw. When her mouth twitched, she swiped her mouth with her hand, both movements done in the same order, in the same way over and over. She made humming sounds and clicking noises with her tongue. It looked like some of these things were controllable, but others were out of her control.

She was having a very difficult time socially. She was pulling her desk away from the other children in the grade one classroom. She always had overblown reactions to things most other children wouldn't worry about. We called her the 'drama queen' because she would become almost 'unhinged' with certain events. At home, she would check the doors at night multiple times, flicking the dead bolt back-and-forth three times, checking the house alarm three times, checking to ensure the windows were locked three times. This routine went on multiple times before she would settle into bed.

Bedtime had always been a challenge but now she was experiencing night terrors regularly. The worst reoccurring night terror was of her dad hanging from the roof outside her window in a noose, face contorted and grey, multiple stab wounds to his torso and his body dripping with blood. It was vivid and terrifying. She told us of other nightmares where myself, her Dad, her siblings and our family dog would perish in some unbelievably violent way. No one was safe in her sleep. I needed help for her. I went to the family doctor, a few pediatric-type doctors; I think we even went to see a psychiatrist once during that time. They gave me no good answers, no support, and I became increasingly frightened for her.

Eventually with the help of a friend and her doctor, I got her to the Toronto Western Tourette's Clinic. Christina was interviewed by a few doctors there. When they spoke to me about her diagnosis, one of them relayed something she said during her interview… Christina told him she wanted to turn her bed over and bang her head on the steel part until she stopped breathing. She was diagnosed by the head doctor there with Tourette's Syndrome, Obsessive Compulsive Disorder, and General Anxiety Disorder.

I had no support for her diagnosis from most of the family and friends I dared to share it with. When I did share, I was met with harsh judgment of my child and myself. I stopped talking to anyone about anything to do with my daughter. Despite the lack of support (and even some protests by people close to me) I continued to seek help and advocate for her at home and school. I just kept doing my own research and saving my questions for the next doctor's appointment at the Tourette's Clinic.

Fast forward to the age of seventeen. Her anxiety and depression had escalated. Looking back at these times, I now realize these great lows had also been followed by highs. After one hugely unpredictable year (which I thought could be the normal emotions of a teenager) she had one specifically long and destructive high. It landed her in the hospital, culminating in her diagnosis: bipolar disorder.

I really needed support and help from others. I could not handle this on my own anymore.

I went to the hospital, friends in the community, her outpatient psychiatrist and asked for a parent support group or parenting course, anything to get me through these times. After searching, I found nothing. As Christina became more stabilized, I realized I need to share my story with the thought that there are other parents out there that feel the same isolation that I can still feel. I'm hoping that these parents will find my podcasts or book of interviews not only comforting, but also supporting. My aim is to create a community of shared experiences with the thought that no parent should feel alone.

Raising a child who is 'different' from the other kids takes a great mental and emotional toll on the parents. They are worn out and pushed to the brink, totally exhausted. Many are tapped-out financially and in some cases they have had to quit their jobs or take lesser ones to be there for the next episode when their child can't cope. There is little or no support from a system caught up in process and willfully lacking in parental resources.

As a parent of a challenging child, you can also brace yourself for the stigma of a lifetime. We look like the accomplice to this very badly behaved, poorly mannered and emotionally unstable child. If you don't have a diagnosis it's worse. If you don't have money it's worse still. So much of what we require to help our children isn't covered by government health insurance plans, like Ontario's OHIP, or by extended health insurance.

The general parent community is unsupportive at best; hostile and judgmental at its worst. This compounds the pain and stress we live through every day. We go through things very few parents can relate to.

This book is a collection of my interviews with kids affected with challenges, parents of those kids, and even medical professionals from the mental health community. In many cases, the name of the child has been changed or last names of the contributors omitted to maintain privacy for themselves and their children.

Access the Audio Interviews

If you like to listen as well as read, all the interviews that this book is based on are available on iTunes, as episodes of my podcast of the same name: *Different from the Other Kids*.

http://www.dftok.com/podcast-info

A Note On Language

The book you are holding in your hands was compiled from transcripts of conversations I held for my podcast. People don't speak the way they write. Spoken language is messy. It goes off in unexpected directions—sometimes in the middle of a sentence.

I have deliberately kept the language in this book as close as possible to the words used in the interview. I wanted to get across not just the message, but also the spirit of the people I have interviewed. As a result, I have only made changes where it was necessary for clarity and understanding. Otherwise, what you are reading is exactly what was said.

The result is a book that doesn't always follow strict rules of structure. It is not a perfect book. But it is a perfect window into the experiences, feelings and thoughts of everyone involved.

Read it and enjoy it. And don't worry about occasional lapses of grammar—there are far more important things to worry about.

Different from the Other Kids

The Day I Found Out I Was Bipolar

In this chapter Angela interviews her own daughter Christina about her experience and feelings about her initial bipolar diagnosis. The extreme struggles of this seventeen year old girl eventually forced her be hospitalized and ultimately led to her being diagnosed with bipolar disorder. They each share their perspectives, how they felt, what they went through leading up to the diagnosis, and what Christina went through during treatment.

This interview was first recorded May, 2013.

Angela: Here I have my daughter Christina with me. Why don't you tell everyone a little bit about yourself, Chrissy?

Christina: Well, I'm twenty years old. I am a certified personal trainer and I graduated from Sheridan College approximately one year ago. I was working at a fitness club for just under two years and then left because I wasn't enjoying the environment. I am currently working for a boating company who carry out maintenance work on boats such as detailing, polishing, waxing and painting. It's a lot of fun. I love being outside, and it's a very good workout, which keeps my emotions really level so it's working out really well.

I am also living at home with my sister, my brother, my mother's partner Melinda, and our beloved dog Scrapper. It's awesome living at home. I love my family. We are all really close.

Angela: I think it's important that everyone know a little bit of who Christina is, from my perspective. I think she is very kind, very sweet, smart, quick thinking and enthusiastic, with a wonderful sense of humour.

One thing I think is important for everyone to know is that Christina works very hard every day to manage her moods and symptoms and she constantly strives to be better than the day before. It's like a marathon for her, because she runs it every day and I think, for the most part, she manages everything really well. She has experienced many different hardships and it would be easy to let them defeat her. Instead she gets back up and on with life, always trying to improve herself. She is a wonderful, loving daughter and a wonderful big sister to her two siblings.

Christina, let's look back and talk about your initial diagnosis. It's a little painful, but there is one particular day that we should share. It was the beginning of the new normal, and it was one of the biggest changes of our lives. Talk us through that day from your perspective.

Christina: I remember that for a couple of weeks I was extremely happy and felt just over the moon. Invincible. That I could do anything. My Mom didn't think anything was wrong. Maybe she might have thought I was acting a little bit too happy—I think she was just really pleased that I wasn't in bed feeling depressed, but was active and enjoying spending time with friends. To the outside world I was acting 'normal', or what society deems as such. Neither of us thought there was anything wrong because no one is ever concerned with someone being happy.

But this one day, there was a trigger. I was being a little bit promiscuous around this time and my mom ended up finding out. She took my car away and was very concerned about how impulsive my actions were. At the time I was really mad at her. I had a complete freak out, got extremely pissed off and decided to take an entire bottle of Prozac that I had been using as antidepressants. I put the bottle in my bag, walked back to school and, right before I walked into school, I took what was left of the bottle of pills and swallowed them.

Angela: Why did you take them? I think that's important to address.

Christina: It was an impulsive reaction. This constant thought of "I just can't do this. Everything is just too much." It was in that moment that I wanted to die. It was an instant reaction to "I can't feel this right now. I just can't feel this, and I'll do anything to not feel this."

Angela: I remember you saying you wanted 'it' to stop: what exactly was it that you wanted to stop?

Christina: I don't know what it was. It's just the overwhelming emotional stress and feelings that came over me; I just wanted it to stop. I haven't felt like that since that incident and I can't really explain myself any more than that. It just feels like you literally can't handle the emotions that you're feeling at that second and the only way to deal with it is to end your life.

That day I had two friends at school who I called before I left the house. I was in tears, just completely freaking out with extreme anger toward my Mom. They met me at the school and they were asking, "What's wrong with you? You look so weird." I couldn't really walk properly, and felt really uncomfortable. They kept asking, "What's going on?"

I told them that I had taken a bottle of pills, and they were in shock. After that, they brought me into the school and we walked through the halls for a little bit until a teacher passed by. At this point they were physically holding me up. The teacher just asked, "Is everything ok?" and Robin, my friend, told the teacher "She just took a bunch of pills." So the teacher brought me down to the guidance office. All I remember is seeing all the guidance counsellors sitting at a table with me. One of the guidance counsellors asked me, "What happened? Why did you do this?" I never really had any answer for her. I was still in shock, and I didn't really know what was going on.

When the ambulance arrived, everyone was really concerned for my well-being and I was escorted by two police officers to the hospital. At this point no one could get in touch with anybody in my family except my sister, who went to the same school as I did. She was in grade nine and I was in grade eleven.

Both of my parents were unreachable at that time: my Dad was out of the country and my Mom wasn't answering her phone. The hospital ended up having to call my Grandmother, who then came to the hospital. By the time my Grandmother arrived at the hospital, the staff still couldn't reach my mom. So, the two police officers stayed with me for hours while I waited to see a psychiatric nurse. I didn't have to get my stomach pumped or anything, thank goodness—it wasn't that serious. I was given some charcoal to coat my stomach, and they monitored me. I was really lucky that I didn't take more medication than I had, otherwise the situation would have been life-threatening.

My Mom finally came to the hospital, and she was furious. I've never seen her so angry at me in my entire life! I was bawling my eyes out thinking "Why is she so mad at me, shouldn't she care more?" Now I know her reaction was because she was so worried, but at the time it just didn't really help that she was so pissed at me.

After that, they took me in to see the psychiatric nurse. She was so sweet. She just asked me a bunch of questions like, "Did you intentionally want to hurt yourself?" At this point, I knew something was wrong. I now know that I was having a complete manic episode. I was a good liar when I was manic, so I told her everything she wanted to hear in order for her to feel confident enough to let me go home.

My Mom begged her to make me stay; begged her to keep me there because she had no idea what the hell to do with me. I thought that I was going home, and then all of a sudden she told me "We're putting you on a seventy-two hour hold." I asked "What does that mean? Do I have to stay here?" and she explained that, legally, I had to stay there for seventy-two hours.

They brought me down to the children's psychiatric wing, as I was under eighteen years old at this point; and I remember sitting with my Mom and the crisis nurse that was there. The nurse was asking me questions in order to admit me, but I was a complete mess and they had to give me a couple of Ativan to calm me down and just sleep.

I ended up getting a roommate who was definitely in a worse spot than I was. She was really hard to deal with. She would have outbursts and other issues, so I kept to myself.

At this point it was still the weekend, so I couldn't see the doctor for two days. Staying there was the worst three weeks of my entire life, but also the best three weeks of my entire life.

Angela: You don't really remember a lot. I do wish I remembered more, but I think that, because it was such a painful experience, I try to focus on the positive.

Christina: It was a couple of days before I got on the medication, but I did see the doctor. I think it was the Saturday or Sunday, and then I saw him right away on the Monday. He started me on several types of medication, but I don't remember what they were.

I do remember one was Lithium, which did not agree with me at all. At this point I was still manic, and whatever I said in my counselling sessions with the counsellors was what they wanted to hear. One day, one of them actually came into the room and said "OK, cut the bullshit. You're telling me everything I want to hear right now. What's going on? You know there's something wrong: why aren't you talking about it?"

At that point, I realized that maybe there was something wrong. Maybe I was just too happy. I think I was actually able to reflect on my behaviour because I had been on a medication called Seroquel for a couple of days. This was when he came into my room, and I wasn't as manic. I thought to myself "Yeah, there is something wrong. No normal person decides to take a whole bottle of pills when they're angry." After that realization, I had counselling for another two to three weeks.

Angela: Which was the better part of the three weeks? Do you want to elaborate on this?

Christina: The better part of the three weeks was when we did a group therapy and had a very rigid schedule. I got a lot of support from my school. My teachers were helping me with my assignments and pushing me to finish. They let me put my assignments together to ensure I got all my credits. The teachers there were awesome. Everybody was awesome.

There were a lot of incidents though at nighttime. A couple of kids would have freak-outs and have to be restrained, so we would have security on the whole floor and go into lockdown. The scariest nights of my life were being locked up in there. Oh my God, it was awful. Just awful. It was so scary, and not having any means of communicating with the outside world was awful.

I remember my Mom coming to visit me, and it was the highlight of my day. But I was still so angry at her for so long that I didn't even know why. We've gotten past that now, though, and things are good.

Dr. Brown was my doctor at Oakville Hospital, and he had diagnosed me as bipolar. He started me on Seroquel—I don't remember how many milligrams of it—but this was after…I think he tried one or two tries, and it seemed to start working. I started feeling less high and a little bit more like myself. I did miss the high.

The high is awesome. But I know the high is absolutely awful, and there is a crash that comes with it, along with consequences for my actions.

After that, I was released after three weeks. I don't remember a lot. I think I was in so much trauma that I just repressed it. I'm surprised I remember as much as I just told you. After I got discharged, I had to meet with a psychiatrist in Oakville.

Angela: Yeah, there was an outpatient psychiatric clinic. There was a doctor there who was referred to us for the pharmaceutical part of it. She did do a little counselling, but not very much. The treatment was more medicine-based.

Christina: I had been seeing a counsellor already for probably four or five years after my parents' divorce. I took the divorce really hard and needed to talk to someone who wasn't my family. After my first manic episode, I started seeing my counsellor weekly. I have now been seeing her for eight years; she's absolutely amazing.

Coming out of the hospital, they got me to write all the goals that I wanted in life and all the things I wanted to achieve—such as where I wanted to be in ten years, where I want to be in five years, and what I wanted to do with my life. I really started thinking about that, and I don't remember a good chunk up until I went to school. I ended up dating someone for about two years and he was a great guy. He was pretty level-headed and kind of kept me balanced through my ups and downs. I know that's exactly what I needed from a partner—stability. There can't be any ups and downs and craziness going on. It has to be completely stable. I don't remember a lot from then. That was also the time I was trying to figure out exactly what was going to work for me, medication-wise, as a lot of medications can make your memory a little fuzzy.

Angela: Yes, but not street drugs.

Christina: Yes, not street drugs, I should have said that. I was on a lot anti-psychotic drugs, so yes, still testing a cocktail of medication that was going to work for me and keep my chemicals level.

Angela: You were level for about eighteen months. I'm going to say it took about six months to even off?

Christina: Six months or so.

Angela: And then you stayed level.

Christina: Yeah, it was a good eighteen months until the next episode came around.

Angela: What was the next episode?

Christina: Oh just recently. It started about a year ago.

Angela: With your other boyfriend. Can you elaborate what triggered your episode?

Just to tell you that is Christina's perspective and then there is my perspective, which isn't that far off. Her behaviour over that particular Christmas was really weird. It got to the point of being odd.

Now, she had gone through long periods of time—for quite a few years actually—where she would be quite depressed. I remember that for a summer—probably three summers before that, or something like that—I could not, for the life of me, get her out of bed. It was a challenge for her to shower, to do anything. We noticed that she was actually dealing with depression, which of course she was. But we didn't realize that there was another element to it. So, during that particular Christmas, what was different was that she was flitting a little bit back and forth from the summer. She seemed to get really kind of weirdly happy, but it wouldn't last for very long, and then she would crash again.

What she has always dealt with, more than the mania, is the depression. So I just thought, "Oh that's good, she's bouncing out of the depression pretty well," and then she would crash again. That's why we were dealing with the antidepressants at that time. Everyone seemed to think it was more depression than anything else. So that's what we were medicating.

What I know now is that when you are on an antidepressant and you are bipolar, you can actually trigger an episode; a completely manic episode. They are misdiagnosed and they end up "disinhibiting". I don't know what the medical part of all of that is but it triggers the brain chemicals in the opposite direction. So, during that period of time she ended up losing the depression entirely. It was probably three weeks of a bit of wildness and completely unlike her.

She's always great when she's level: she's always enthusiastic, usually quite happy, she's easy to get along with and that kind of stuff. But what she started three weeks before was a quickening in her speech, and she was running around a bit too much. She had gotten a car in the fall and was just constantly in and out of the house. This escalated for that three-week period that led us up to the day that she was at school and the ambulance had to be called.

It had gotten to the point within the last five days before the day of hospitalization, that I was very worried. It seemed that she was going off in a bunch of different directions and was not able to even finish a thought, never mind finish a task. She would be in the middle of something and get up, and all of a sudden she had to go out in the car. Then she would come back and there would be this blast of energy. She wouldn't finish whatever it was that she was saying, and she would go out. There was a strange look on her face; a very intense look in her eyes.

Christina: Crazy eyes. Sometimes I ask, when I'm feeling high, if I have the 'crazy eyes'.

Angela: Christina does get to the point where she can recognize the feeling of being manic, as well as some of those other symptoms. You get to the point where you start to not be able to sit still. There is a bit of pattern finding. Trying to figure out whether there is actually a manic episode happening. The other part of being bipolar is depression. That's not hard to spot, but it happens in varying degrees. Things like she can't get out of bed; everything is too exhausting. Doing the most mundane task—like getting up in the morning and showering—just feels overwhelming for a person who is depressed. They are very low; everything feels like a personal affront; usually, everything feels devastating. They can read a lot into what you are saying, sometimes seeing it as too negative or extreme. They constantly assume it's directed at them, when that's certainly not the intention.

That particular day was concerning me. I had gotten to a point where I was worried enough about her, and her extreme behaviour, that I then looked at her and I said, "I am so sorry" and this was first thing in the morning. I said "I am so sorry Christina, until I figure out what is going on with you and where your head is at, I need to take these car keys from you." I said, "I'm going to keep them. If you need a ride somewhere let me know, but whatever it is you're going through right now is worrying me: I'm afraid to have you behind the wheel."

I knew that she was upset when she left, but I had no idea just to what extent. I didn't think that this was going to be any kind of a problem.

So she went to school and I was exhausted. I had been dealing with her and trying to deal with what was happening with her. I was mystified. As a parent you tend to get very tired: from the constant worrying, the fact you're dealing with too much, there are incidents happening and strange behaviours.

I will tell you, it gets exhausting trying to deal with this person; trying to ground them and trying to keep them safe; trying to see if they are eating; trying to see what it is they are saying. They seem to have all these little side conversations going on at different times. There's so much of the time when they don't seem to be telling the truth, even though this person that you know and love is truthful by nature. They are not liars, but there's all this stuff going on that is really making you question what's happening.

After she left for school, I was so exhausted that I had to lie down because I was very upset. I remember the phone ringing a few times.

I can't remember how many calls there were—maybe four? I had been trying to nod off to sleep but couldn't, so it was probably on the fifth call that I picked up. It was the school principal calling to say that Christina had been taken by ambulance because she had taken a bottle of pills, and that I needed to meet her at the hospital.

I called her therapist at the time ... I didn't have time to call anyone else. Then my Mom called me as I was getting into my car, saying that she was leaving to go to the hospital because they had called her. I said "OK, thank you." My Mom ended up getting there before me. When I walked in, I saw Christina on a stretcher. You could tell she had been crying and there were two police officers with her as she wasn't allowed to be alone. She had already been seen by the psychiatric nurse, and my Mom was sitting at the bottom of Christina's bed in the hallway. I was absolutely devastated.

There is no way to fully describe what that feels like for a parent, and I can tell by Christina's face right now that there is no way to describe what that look on my face was. I wasn't able to properly process what happened, so what I had was whatever my go-to-feeling was at the time. Yeah, I was angry. I couldn't talk and I could barely look at her. I was so upset, and she just kept saying "I'm so sorry. I'm so sorry." As I looked at her I asked "What in the world would ever possess you to do this?" and she just shook her head, saying "I just wanted to make it stop."

I didn't know what that meant at the time, but I think I do know now. She wanted to stop the thoughts that were racing through her head. She wanted to stop the things that were happening around her; the things that she was making happen; the things that weren't really "her". She wasn't comfortable in her own skin and she was trying to make it stop. So no, I didn't react very well. I'm sorry about that Chrissy.

Christina: That's OK Mom, I understand now that we both didn't know what was going on.

Angela: Yeah, so I was there for a couple of hours probably. I sat there with my Mom. Nobody said a thing. My Mom and I looked at one another, and the shattered look on my Mother's face, too, was part of why I guess it was so difficult. Eventually we were seen by the psychiatric nurse, who was exceptional. She talked to Christina and I in one of the isolation rooms; one of the rooms with the glass.

It was four walls and a steel door. The nurse was amazing. She asked us a lot of different questions about how Christina had been feeling; about what led her to this. And she looked at me and said "Well she doesn't seem like she wants to take her life right now. There is something called a three-day psychiatric hold, but I'm just not sure we're really ready for it at this point." And I looked at her and said "You have got to help me. I am a mother. I'm the only parent in the house. I have no idea. I do not have a clue how to deal with this kid right now."

I said "Her behaviour is so out of the realm of what is ordinary for her, I'm afraid she's going to do something further. I'm afraid she's going to do something more severe than what she has done. I am lost. I have no idea what to do. I am begging you to please keep her. I need to figure out what is going on with her, and she needs to be in a safe place because I can't make her safe."

And I think I said that a few times. "I just can't make her safe. I can't. I can't do it." So the psychiatric nurse looked at me, and right away nodded her head and there was a three-day psychiatric hold.

Taking Christina into that unit was very difficult as well, because there is a lot of security. They are young people there. I can't remember how many beds were there—I think there might have been enough for ten kids. The staff were exceptional, but they were very strict. When we went in to say good night to her, they were going through her personal belongings. I had to take most items back home with me, such as shoestrings and any sharp objects, like a pen. She basically had nothing; just the clothes on her back. I was able to bring in one pillow, a blanket and one pair of pajamas. They took the draw string out of the boxers, which was delightful!

I will tell you that Christina and I both believe at this point that the three-day hold absolutely saved her life. I believe it to be one of the greatest things that ever happened to us. She was able to get treatment right away; a diagnosis right away; the proper drug treatment right away; and learn some coping skills.

They didn't just keep her for the three days. Once the psychiatrist saw her and thought he had a diagnosis, he asked if he would be able to keep her further. She agreed, which was fantastic and amazingly grown up of her—especially during that time, because she was still quite manic.

I can't say it enough: absolutely the greatest thing that ever happened to us, was her staying in that facility and getting some of the tools that she was going to need to go forward with for the rest of her life.

Christina is an exceptional young person and very brave for trying to get help. Her ability to tell the absolute, raw truth demonstrates the courage of the person that we're talking about here. I want to share a quote that she wrote on Facebook a couple of months ago, that I think speaks to who she is.

Christina: It's one of my favourite quotes. I found this quote on Instagram. It says "I'm in competition with no one. I run my own race. I have no desire to play the game of being better than anyone in any way, shape or form. I just aim to improve. To be better than I was before."

Angela: Parents, I'm hoping that this was a bit enlightening or perhaps it makes you feel less alone. Perhaps it gives you some kind of hope. That's the aim, it's to give you something to hold onto for some of those days that are a little more difficult.

Breaking-Up Is Hard To Do

In this chapter, Angela interviews her daughter Christina about her second big bipolar episode. She discusses the triggers that caused the episode, with both of their sides of the story and how they handled the situation. They get really in-depth into what goes on in the mind of a person with bipolar disorder during such a traumatic time.

This interview was first recorded June, 2013.

Angela: Hello I'm here today interviewing my daughter Christina. Let me tell you a little bit about my beautiful 'bipolar' daughter. She is not bipolar. She is a person who has a bipolar disorder: that's an important distinction. She is a wonderful human being. She is working full-time presently, which is very exciting. She is working outside, which has been a fantastic thing for her, as she receives nature's light therapy, water therapy and a solid day of hard physical work. She's cleaning and detailing boats and is having a really great time doing it.

It has been difficult for her to work in the last few months, so this is a really great opportunity for her and she's doing exceptionally well.

Something else to know about Christina is that when she is doing well, she's a wonderful, charismatic, charming young woman. She's very enthusiastic, a fast learner, and she's got a great sense of humour. She is running a marathon here with her moods, and I think she's doing a great job of trying to manage her symptoms all the time. She is trying to do all the things that are necessary to keep herself stable. I think Christina is meant to do great things in her life but that isn't always as easy as it seems when dealing with bipolar disorder.

We discussed her first serious episode in our last interview, and today we will talk to her about her second episode. This takes a lot of courage and a lot of guts, and I take my hat off to you Chrissy: this is raw stuff to talk about.

Christina: The last time we spoke I was giving you background on how I was diagnosed and the events leading up to that. After I left the hospital, I had great tools and left feeling really confident.

I also had a great support system at home. I was set up with a psychiatrist and a counsellor, and seemed to be on a set of meds that was really working for me. I was really good! I had a really good relationship. I was still young, but I was seeing someone and he was absolutely amazing and very stable. And at the time, a stable relationship is exactly what I needed. Then we broke up and for about eighteen months, and I was solid. Absolutely solid.

Things were going really well. I was stable, but of course I had a little bit of mania here and there. Some days were a little lower than others, but I didn't have a full blown episode in eighteen months: I really kept my triggers at bay.

Angela: Let me just explain what a trigger is to those who may not know. Triggers can be: a lack of sleep; a difficult relationship; a bully; a situation in life that she doesn't quite know how to deal with, such as an argument. Personal events aren't the only triggers, as sometimes a world event can even trigger an episode. The triggers are endless, and usually result from a situation or circumstance that is beyond the person's control or acceptance.

Christina: As a person with bipolar, you want to make sure that you avoid your triggers, if at all possible. I was doing really well and coping through therapy, counselling and my support system. I had just started school. I was at Sheridan College studying to be a personal trainer, which I absolutely loved, but it was really stressful and that was a huge trigger for me as well. With school I stress out really easily; I get overwhelmed; and I was taking an advanced course to graduate faster. It was a lot of work, and there was a lot of new information in combined sciences, which wasn't my strong suit. I was still working part-time at GoodLife Fitness while I was in school, hoping that I would get a job right out of college.

After breaking up with 'Mr. Stable', I had met a new guy and things were going really well. I fell in love with him right away. I do believe to this day that he was my first love. I was loving school, and I had a job waiting for me at GoodLife Fitness as a full-time personal trainer. I knew exactly what I wanted to do. I could help people in all the ways that I wanted to, and I had also lost almost one hundred pounds by just loving myself, eating well and exercising.

I can't stress enough just how important exercise and nutrition are to keep you stable for so long. I can't say it enough: exercise, exercise, exercise, exercise. I notice a difference in my day when I don't do something physical. So I can't stress that enough. Definitely get your children moving. Even walking: just going for walks and releasing endorphins is a huge deal.

Things started getting a little rocky between my boyfriend and me. I had started working full-time at the gym. It was a full-time job, which my psychiatrist, my counsellor and everyone were absolutely amazed that I was able to handle. The hours were insane, because as a personal trainer you start at 6 a.m. and your last client finishes at 9 p.m. It was stressful, my sleep routine was off and the sales pressure was a lot to deal with. My mood started to fluctuate, and things weren't going well with my boyfriend. We had a really intense relationship, and there was a big difference in what each of us wanted out of the relationship. It should have ended a lot earlier than it did. Between my job and my relationship, things started to spiral. Those are two huge factors that influenced my next episode.

Angela: Can you walk us through what that looks like: the disintegration that I am hoping that you saw as clearly as I did.

Christina: I began to notice myself hating work: it was hard to get out of bed in the morning; I wasn't enjoying it and I would come home at night feeling grumpy and sad; I was just low all the time; I was constantly calling my clients and cancelling on them. Everything started falling apart around me. I used to love the gym, and I just almost completely stopped working out. I began to stop loving the things that I used to love.

Angela: How long did it take for that spiral to bottom out?

Christina: I was a personal trainer for seven months. I would say for the first three months I did not have that many clients, as it takes a while to accumulate them at the beginning. For the first three months it was great; I was doing well. Boyfriend problems were still there, but work was great. It wasn't until work kind of shifted that I decided to leave my job.

At the time, I thought that was the best move for me. I am very lucky that I had my parents to support me: I'm still living at home and they're absolutely amazing. My Mom saw what the job was doing to me. She was all for it and said "You know what? You need a clean, fresh slate. This is not working for you. Let's call it as it is: you are a mess."

So I left work and I was a little better after that. Not having to work the crazy hours and not having all of that responsibility and constant pressure to sell. Things got a little better. I started just working out a little bit more again and ended the relationship I was in.

We broke up many times. Every time it was the most devastating thing I had ever gone through. From the outside looking in, it may have looked like someone had died because of how hysterical I got. He was killing me; absolutely killing me. It wasn't even like I was sad. It was like "Someone may as well kill me now, because I can't deal with the pain."

There was a night when he was out with his friends. He was drunk and I was trying to talk to him and he wasn't having any of it. We were broken up at this point, and he basically told me it was over and he couldn't deal with me anymore. My Mom had already taken my medication away from me, because that night I was such a mess. It was 2 o'clock in the morning, and I went into her room and grabbed another bottle of pills, intending to down the whole bottle. She woke up and was so mad at me that she took me back to the hospital.

It was different this time because I knew the consequences, but I just couldn't handle the emotions anymore. I couldn't handle the emotion I was feeling. I just thought "I need out. I just can't feel this pain. This pain is too much."

I know a lot of people don't understand, and I am sure parents of bipolar kids don't understand that pain; that overwhelming, sickeningly awful pain that someone with a mental illness would feel. But I can tell you it's the worst thing in the world, and I really hope that you try to understand that for them.

It's not a choice. It's not that you're consciously saying "Yes I want to die." It's the fact that there is no other option but to make this pain go away.

In ten days we were at the hospital three times. The third was the most intense. My Mom was seriously at the end of her rope, and told me she had to check me in and leave me there. The psychiatric nurse wasn't there, so they were waiting for the doctor who was on call. It was a weekend, so there is no psychiatrist or anybody like that on shift.

When he came in, I was exhausted. I had taken my medication earlier that night so it was kicking in and I could barely stay awake. I remember not wanting to ever feel like this again. I told my Mom I didn't want to actually kill myself. In that moment, before we went to hospital, I truly don't know if I would have taken the pills or not. I don't think I would have. I think, honestly, I went in there to wake my Mom up because I needed help. Sometimes it's the most dramatic, absolutely insane cry for help that you could ever do. It's absolutely ridiculous, but at the time there's nothing else you're thinking. I wish I could have just woke her up and said "Mom, I really need you", instead of causing this huge scene and having her drag me to the hospital at 2.30 a.m. in the morning. The fact is, it needed to be done. The thought of having to stay in that hospital jolted me back to some reality. It began to occur to me that it was sickening to think about hurting myself because of a bad breakup.

After some time, I did end up getting back together with him again, after all that. I'm happy to say that now we are not together, and I am free and ten times more stable. Stable now that I'm not with him, I guess I should say.

Now, I have a job where I'm working full-time and its outside; it's physical. It's all the good therapies that they always say that you need. This is probably the fifth or sixth week that I have been better and productive every day. That episode lasted a long time, but I found a good balance of new medication that I'm on.

I'm on Latuda, which is a new type of anti-psychotic drug that hasn't really been tested on someone as young as I am. It's working absolutely amazingly. I'm also on Wellbutrin, which has anti-depressive properties and is a stimulant to keep me up instead of low, because I am usually more down than up.

Angela: From my perspective as a parent, over the last twelve months it has been the most excruciating thing to watch someone go through. The sobbing and crying to the point of sounding guttural; it's like an animal pain. You would absolutely have thought that somebody had died right in front of her every time she dealt with another break up with her now ex-boyfriend.

What I think that is important for you to know and understand, is that when people see Christina when she is well, they always tell me what a lovely, charming human being she is.

When she was at GoodLife Fitness, she sold like nobody else sold on the floor. She had people coming in just to train with her. She was always optimistic, always positive, knew her stuff, was able to connect with people in a way that most people just can't. She is old beyond her years, and probably in part that's because of what she has experienced. She actually understands people in a different way because she's been in the darkest depths of the human experience.

Very few people believe that this unstable person I speak of is Christina. They couldn't even imagine her like that. They say things like "That doesn't sound right. Are you sure you got the diagnosis right?" You name it, they have asked it, because when she's stable, she's a fantastic force. She has jobs and opportunities come her way all the time. That's who she is and that's not a manic state. Her actual regular everyday state is that dependable, wise person. I just want you to think about that as we talk through the disintegration process when she is having an episode.

When she got home three weeks after the initial hospitalization, she did bounce back and forth for about six months. I remember very clearly that she had been quite manic one particular night and saying that I needed to help her.

I know she doesn't remember. There's a lot that she doesn't remember and a lot that I don't remember, so bear in mind that this is natural when dealing with such traumatic situations. I remember her behaviour was going 'sideways' a bit again. There were days that medication would be working, and then some days that it wasn't working well. I said "You've got a brother and a sister in this house, and you have turned it completely upside down. This is not fair to them and it's not fair to me, and I don't want to live like this." Then I just very plainly said "Do you like living here?" And she looked at me with this shock and awe and she asked, "What do you mean?" And I said "Do you like living here? There are other options." I felt terrible saying that, but there comes a point when, as the parent, you have to take some control back in an uncontrollable situation. She has a responsibility to the people that absolutely love and adore her, that are constantly around her. She needed to make sure that she took some responsibility in getting well. She needed to know, regardless of whether she was mentally 'off' or not.

I told her that there were some outpatient programs and residential treatment programs that I could send her to, but that I really didn't want to. I told her that I was really hoping that she was going to start participating in her own rescue and figuring out what she needed to do to stabilize. It was from there, and with the help of a counsellor, that Christina started making some really great changes. There were big changes from the medication, the counselling, the med checking with the psychiatrist, and the fitness and nutrition. Fitness in and of itself is medicine, and we began to look at it as such.

You absolutely have to stick to a fitness regimen. It can be anything, such as walking, and many people with mental illness run, weight lift, play basketball, any kind of racket sport: they just have to get out there and really move. There are people out there that can do half an hour to keep stable if they go hard enough. Other people with certain amounts of anxiety will need to go much longer. It all depends on your mood and physical capabilities.

It was for about eighteen months that Christina was fantastic, even back to her regular self; you would never have known that anything had happened to change things for her. Over that period of time, through fitness and exercise, she lost about eighty-five pounds. She was in therapy doing the counselling and then decided to go to college. College was very difficult, but she loved it. She was there eight months, and she did pretty darn well all the way through until the last six weeks of school. We got her a tutor who was amazing. She actually really helped with all of the overwhelm and workload.

Margaret was wonderful. Christina couldn't sit still: there was only so much that she could listen to; she had to get up and walk around the halls in the middle of class; she was always moving in her seat. It could be a side effect of the medication—I'm really not sure. It was from that initial diagnosis that she really was fidgety and had a hard time sitting still.

At the same time as she was going to school, she was working part-time. She had two or three different positions at the end of that job within a short period of time (about a year). There was a lot of stimulation, lots of different personalities and the hours were difficult to handle. What we know for sure is this: fitness, nutrition and structure work. I don't know if I can put them in that order exactly, but structure is part of the drill, and not having it was really messing with Christina's ability to cope. She was getting up really early in the morning and then wasn't able to unwind in the evening.

She worked well into the evening some nights. She couldn't get her meals made.

The last six weeks of school were a really difficult time. She was getting depressed; she wasn't eating right, and instead was eating for comfort. At the same time, she was starting to gain a little bit of weight, which made her really uncomfortable. This great job, that she did so well, became unmanageable and unfortunately she had to give it up. They loved her there, but towards the end it was very difficult for her to show up, and when she did show up she was completely anxiety-ridden and freaked-out.

Then the breakup with her first love was extremely devastating for her. As the breakups got closer and closer together, she completely unravelled. It's terrible watching this kid deteriorate in front of your eyes and no matter what you do, you can't seem to pull them back together. There was about a ten day period there where we had to get into a full suicide watch. Christina wasn't to be on her own. She was with me 24/7.

Christina: I wasn't allowed to have a phone either.

Angela: I took away her phone for a little bit so that she wasn't in contact with that person. It would take one text and she would be thrown off for twenty-four hours or thirty-six hours. It's exhausting doing this for her, and it's exhausting as a parent trying to help her through it. We were together every moment of the day for probably a month. Every single day. 24/7.

It's hard. As a parent you are trying to manage her, she's trying to manage herself and it's really difficult. We would watch TV, go for a walk, get pedicures, manicures, go out for yogurt; she would come with me to the office; we would go work out. I just tried to keep her moving. The ten days of full-on suicide watch was horrifying. I was constantly checking-in with her therapist—who is just an outstanding woman—who actually allowed me to keep in constant contact with her, which is not typical. Her therapist did home visits during that period of time, which was extraordinary.

Not a soul in my life would have understood what I was going through. No one wanted to listen to what was happening. I think it's a lot for people to process. For the parent dealing with it all the time, it is beyond stressful. There is no refuge, and no downtime to take a breath or have a cry.

During that ten day period, Christina went into the hospital three different nights. She kept saying she wanted to die, she didn't want to be here anymore, she'd be better off dead. When you hear those kinds of things, you don't take them lightly. We would be there at all different hours, waiting for a nurse to see us. The nurse would have to refer us to the doctor on-call, and we would have to wait longer.

Each time, they released her to me, but each time they asked if I could handle her. Her rap sheet at the hospital would say she was depressive and suicidal. Each time I took her to the hospital, she would come out of soul-shattered state to a small degree. "Mommy, I promise I'm not going to hurt myself. I promise I'm going to get better. I promise I'm not going to hurt myself. Please don't leave me here. Please don't. Please don't leave me here again. I can't ever come back to this place. I can't ever be under lockdown with those people again."

The last episode, I really thought I was leaving her there that night. She had wrestled me for the pills in the middle of the night. I was mad, but allowing myself to get that angry would sometimes shock her out of it. It's not pretty, but it can work. It also comes with a price. They remember how angry you were and how non-empathetic you came across to them at that time.

That night, I knew I needed to do something, if only to get her to the hospital. I had to get her stable enough, shocked enough, that I could get her into the car to get her some help. I really didn't want to have to call an ambulance. I didn't know if they would restrain her if she was uncooperative, but I couldn't take the chance. She was in a very fragile state.

That last night in the hospital she promised to be better, in a way that she hadn't promised in the last ten days. She came home that night. It was still difficult for many days, but she did start to get a little better. She did get back together with the boyfriend again, which was catastrophic when it ended. But that last break was a good one. She came out of it with great understanding, great acceptance of what was happening, and great responsibility for how she needed to deal with it. She's been really on an up-swing ever since.

How long were you on the couch for and glued to the bed, do you remember?

Christina: Three or four weeks, but in those very low, depressed times it often feels like longer. That's why it is important to try and keep yourself busy doing things, even if you think you can't: just try a little bit every day.

Angela: It felt like a long time. It was full-on depression. I couldn't get her to do anything and then the job opportunity came up. I suggested it to her psychologist who thought it was fantastic and now we're bumping along well again. She's done really well and I'm proud of you, Christina! I hope this gives parents listening, some kind of solace, some kind of help, and some kind of hope. Sharing is one way for all of us to stop feeling so isolated and alone.

Christina: For all those people out there struggling with a mental illness, whether it is bipolar disorder, anxiety or depression just remember: "Courage does not always roar. Sometimes it's the quiet voice at the end of the day saying, 'I will try again tomorrow.'"

Angela: That is very much Christina's life: having to get up every day and try and manage this big herculean task and she's winning; at this point we're doing really well.

Christina: Winning!

Never A Victim, But Forever A Fighter

In this chapter, we see a more personal side to Angela, as she interviews her daughter Christina about her bipolar disorder. Christina tells us about her own techniques that help her stay balanced in everyday life.

This interview was first recorded July, 2013.

Angela: Christina has bipolar disorder and what we want to talk about today is how to manage your life with this type of diagnosis. Medication and therapy are two of the things. I want to talk a little bit more about fitness. Fitness, for you in particular and for many in general, is a medicine. I see your whole self get brighter when you are physically active. So let's start from the beginning and talk about medication: when, how and if you should take it.

Christina: OK, I have always been really good about my medication. I know that for some people it's extremely difficult, and I understand a hundred percent why. A lot of the time you don't feel like yourself on your meds; it can make you feel spacey; it kind of feels like an out of body experience. But I know how important it is to take them: they are what keep you sane. When I think about medication I think about not only myself but the people around me, who love me and care about me, they are what keep me going. Ask yourself, "If I wasn't taking the medication right now, how hard would this be on my family?" That's just a little step, a little tool that you can use, and you can't be selfish and not take it. You have to realize that although you're trying to save yourself, you're also saving the people that care about you.

Taking your medication is the key to have a successful relationship with a partner, to have a successful relationship with your parents, with your siblings, with your friends, with your co-workers, with anybody. Taking it at the same time is huge: the more consistent you can be with it, the better it will work. It's meant to be taken at the same time every day, whether it's morning, whether it's night, whether it's two times a day, whether it's three times a day: take it at the same time each day. I mean half an hour late is not a big deal, but it needs to be within that half an hour.

Keep an extra container with you in your car or wherever you're going so you know you have it. Set an alarm. I have set alarms tons of times to remind myself to take it before I go to bed. I think I have missed medication once just because I completely forgot. Other than that, I have never not taken my medication. Not once. And that one time when I didn't take it, the next day was awful.

Angela: Christina is excellent at taking her medication. I think, too, it's probably the most important thing that she can do for herself. From the beginning she has always been very diligent about it. As a parent I would have to say the most important thing is just make sure that you listen, especially if they're going on a new drug regimen. We had to start a new one just about a year ago. Christina was having a difficult time; her mental state was deteriorating. You have to really listen and pay attention to how they are reacting to a medication. Your observations can be really important for the psychiatrists. I always do my best to go with her to the psychiatrist.

The psychiatrist didn't do much psychotherapy; it was mostly a pharmacological consult. She had to go to the hospital to the outpatient clinic, which means going into a very busy environment and meeting a new doctor. Her anxiety was very high, and she was pretty unstable so I was glad to go with her the first time. I continued to go because the psychiatrist wanted me to. It helps her get a complete picture of how Christina is doing.

Christina: Oh, absolutely. You would have a clearer view of it because I get wrapped up in it myself. Sometimes you will say, "Oh yeah, you were a little manic." And I'll reply, "Really? I didn't even notice." It's good for the parents to keep an eye on what's going on, see how the person is feeling, what moods are showing up, how often it changes and reporting the stuff that is out of character—it's really helpful for me.

Angela: I think it's really important for the psychiatrist as well, because they get the full picture and it allows me to get feedback on what is happening. When Christina hits a "crash" and goes dark, or when the mania hits, or coming in and out of any episode, her thought process is skewed and she doesn't remember everything. We have been very fortunate and we haven't had to go through a ton of medications. We figure out what is working—and what isn't—faster between the two of us. I think it has a lot to do with getting both perspectives, because Christina could explain what she was experiencing and I told them what I was worried about.

She has recounted things when she has been in a difficult state at times, which to me weren't quite true. She wasn't meaning to not be truthful: that was her recollection, and my recollection was different. So I think it really helped. I think we've had better results than most people, being a team.

Angela: Let's talk about the importance of having somebody to talk to.

Christina: Oh my God! Therapy, therapy, therapy, therapy. If you can find a good counsellor or therapist it will help tremendously! There are a lot of things that you can't talk about with people you are close with, whether it be private things or things they just don't really feel comfortable talking to you about. But no matter how young they are, they are still their own individual and will struggle with their individual things that they may not be comfortable sharing with you. Having that outside person's perspective is huge. They can coach you through things. My therapist has helped me with so many coping skills. I learn so much from her. It's like having just one person who just gets it. I've been seeing her for eight years now. The psychotherapist deals with issues on a daily basis, so they will understand it better than most people will. Not to the full extent, of course, but they do empathize and really try to understand with what they have learned through school.

I think it's great for families to do counseling, I know my Mom stepped into a couple of sessions with my therapist just to talk about some things. There are times when it's hard between the parents and the bipolar child, because the parents will try to tell the child to do one thing and the kid wants to do another. There will be times the parents are not understanding of how the child feels and the child's not understanding how the parents feel. Having that extra outside person to talk it through and clarify "This is what she's saying", really helps mediate things and explains the bigger picture.

Making sure that it's regular is another huge thing. I know there have been times when I haven't had an appointment booked and I hit an emergency. Luckily for me, my therapist is very good and has emergency spots available. She leaves room for emergencies on her calendar, but not all counsellors do that.

Having my therapist for regular appointments is the very best thing. When you need to see the counsellor weekly, see them weekly. When you need to see them bi-weekly, see them bi-weekly. But make sure that there is a schedule in place, because they are your go-to crisis person, especially when your parents just don't get it.

Angela: From a parenting perspective, having the right counselor for your child or young adult is integral. I can get really tired of trying to teach the everyday coping skills, and I don't do it nearly as well as Liana can do it. Liana is a fresh and trusted voice that Christina knows is on her side. It's all about her, all the time. The skills that she has taught her range from structure and timing, to dealing with overload or certain personalities. Almost anything and everything you can think of, that there is no rulebook written for in life, Liana has taught Christina some strategy for.

Christina: She also taught me how to deal with my triggers.

Angela: Yes! That is gigantic for people with bipolar disorder! Triggers: figuring out what they are, how to deal with them. That has been part of her therapy as well.

Christina: The deal is, if you want to avoid the triggers you need to know what they are.

Angela: And triggers are everywhere. And it can be almost anything.

Christina: Small things. It can literally be the smallest thing.

Angela: It's a layered process to try and figure out what it is that can set them off. A good therapist will be able to pull that out of your child. I know I'm very fortunate and feel like I have won the lottery with Liana. She has allowed me to have some conversations with her so she can coach me at times when Christina is going through a difficult time. There have been times that I have just texted her and it's nothing but a rant. I'm not actually asking her for anything. I rant that I'm scared to death. I rant about all the things I am doing to get Christina moving. I rant that I don't know if I can do this anymore.

As Christina says, it's just about having somebody on the other side to listen, who might have a clue what I am feeling. She has never betrayed Christina. She is a lifeline for both of us. I know when Christina is going through a hard time, I can send her a text of what is going on and I might get, "Yes, maybe it's time to take her to a hospital." "Have you tried getting Christina to go for a walk?" She just kind of holds my head together at different times, and I know she does for Christina too.

If you were to take on one more thing to keep your symptoms down and your head straight, what would it be? So we have talked about medication and therapy, what else is at the top?

Christina: There are a couple of things. Number one would definitely be fitness and exercise; living a healthy lifestyle. Not only is there a lot of great chemical stuff that goes on when you work out, which has been 100% scientifically proven; it's how it makes me feel. There is also a difference when I'm vigorously working out and when I'm lightly working out. When I lightly work out I feel good, pretty stable. But when I'm vigorously working out I feel completely myself. It's amazing.

When I was heavily weight training, I was at the gym probably an hour and a half to two hours a day working vigorously. I was so stable with regular hard exercise, I can't express that enough. My mood was great. I was happy but not too happy and I never was really sad. And there would be a day where I would miss the workout and I wouldn't feel great, but I wouldn't feel terrible. But if I missed two days I would feel absolutely awful.

Right now, I am more lightly working out, which is why I'm glad I found a job where I'm working that is extremely physical so it's helping to keep my mood stable. My advice is to find a physical job or an after-school activity, or just go for a thirty minute walk every day. That will make a huge difference in your mood.

Add in good nutrition, eat well and cut out those simple sugars (they are toxic for our bodies). Eat lots of vegetables, lots of lean meats, lots of fish, and some beans. Definitely educate yourself on healthy eating and educate yourself on some exercise. The best thing my Mom ever did was to get me a personal trainer. They taught me how to work out properly and safely, because if you're not going to be doing it right then there is no point in doing it. You're not going to get the benefits from the workout that you want without proper form. I believe 100% that vigorously working out will change your state completely.

One more thing I wanted to say, for a lot of bipolar people—I actually haven't had the privilege to meet more than one or two; I'm going to say privilege because it's a privilege to meet other people that are like me—I have noticed there is a lack of confidence, a lack of self-esteem. A lot of you guys think that you're less than other people. You don't think people get you because you have this illness; that you're not worth anything. A lot of times people get settled down into depression and you actually feel sorry for yourself. I've been there a hundred times, but what we have to realize is that you have to look at it as a gift, because no one will feel the good things in life the way you do. There are ups to this, there are downs to this. But it is what it is, and you have to look at it as a gift because it makes you completely different from anybody else; in a good way and in a bad way. Through fitness and physical activity you will be more stable. Your confidence will go up, which will make you happy.

Angela: We had to start with walking and then we graduated to going to the gym. I think you started to do a couple of group classes. I've always been very physically active. I myself used to be a personal trainer and a fitness instructor. Not so much in the last few years. I've been injured and not able to do as much as I would like to. I came from that background and for many years as the kids were growing up, I was involved in fitness as a part-time career. So it was natural for me to get Christina into the gym and to get the other two kids into the gym.

When she was really mentally struggling, I wanted her to get the motivation and the camaraderie of having somebody there, but also somebody that knew what they were talking about to teach proper form. I believe that everyone should learn those basics. Every single kid should learn them. It should be part of a curriculum to learn to perform a weight workout without hurting yourself. Let's teach what cardiovascular activity is, what heart rate is, what the different kinds of cardiovascular activity are. We should be teaching that in school gym programs at a young age. I went through the expense of getting a personal trainer for each of my kids, but Christina had training for probably double the time of the other guys. She needed a bit more of a hand. She was eighty pounds too heavy and really needed the motivation.

Nutrition is harder to learn, but there are some really basic elements that you can integrate into your life that make a great difference to anybody's mental health. It is especially impactful for anyone who has chemical imbalances. As a parent, the best way to help is by getting in the right groceries. Have them prepare it, and you make sure that you have the ingredients. They need to be able to participate in the process so that they learn early on the skills they will need for the rest of their life. If it is at all possible, cut up, clean and get everything ready for them to put together. Give them a head start to try and figure all this stuff out. You have to jump in a little bit in order to support and in order to teach, but they need to learn it in their own time and at their own pace.

Christina: I just want to say on that note of personal training, if you can afford it, absolutely one hundred, thousand percent! I do know that they are a lot of gyms that offer starter packages for personal training. They offer orientations, different types of stuff.

Take them and get them into exercise classes. There are always alternatives, so don't just think that if you can't have personal training then you can't workout, there are tons of alternatives that they could do.

Angela: Well I think if you check out the Internet, if you're in a situation that you certainly could not afford a personal trainer, nor can you afford a gym membership; there are lots of things that you can do outside, such as hiking, running, walking, doing a whole bunch of other things that won't cost you any money. Recreation centres are excellent as well.

OK is there anything else that you want to add, in terms of how you manage?

Christina: Sleep is huge component as well. Routine, sleep and structure: I will touch on those. In terms of sleep, I cannot stress enough the huge difference in my mood when I get my seven to eight hours. There's a huge difference when I get anything less than that. Even if I get nine hours it's awesome. I need a lot of sleep as a person to function. I know everybody needs a different amount, but if you know what your amount of sleep is to function, then work with that and organize yourself to attain that amount of rest.

I notice a huge difference in my mood. It's frustrating in the morning when you wake up and you're actually a little low. Things trigger you a lot more easily when you're sleep deprived. You should be getting your prescribed amount of sleep. For me it's eight to nine hours, one hundred percent. I function best on that. I'm happy with that. And my anxiety, too: it's completely different if I get enough sleep.

Different from the Other Kids

Structure: I have gone through different periods of not having any structure, or having too much structure, and having the perfect amount of structure. Not enough structure will slide you right into depression. You need to be waking up around the same time every day and going to bed around the same time every night. It helps to sync with your medication, which goes with how much sleep you obtain every night. They're all things one should plan.

Structure and making sure you eat at the same time every day. It keeps everything working properly. You can also look into all the scientific theory about why it is good for your body to eat at the same time every day. In short, these tactics help regulate your body.

Angela: When you had great structure, that was the best you have ever felt.

Christina: That's the best I've ever felt, one hundred percent. There will always be challenges like that. They are going to have slip-ups. I'm just getting back on track now after a couple months of completely falling off the wagon. My getting back to structure has been amazing for me.

Again, even though the hours are hard, slowing down a little bit now is nice. With structure I'm ten times happier, and ten times less depressed, than I am when I have no structure. Having no structure means depression. That's all I can really say to that. Having structure creates happiness.

Angela: Sleep is huge. One of the things you will hear me say, even on a weekend, which is really hard for young person is "When did you get to sleep last night?" "Well I was at a party…"

You know what? They need to go out and socialize and do regular stuff. They need to go and have a party with their friends and not drink too much, and certainly never do any drugs because that will never end well. But if they are going to go out with their friends until 1 o'clock in the morning, I know full well she is not going to feel the greatest the next day. Her whole day is shot from trying to make up for the fact that she lost two hours' sleep.

As far as the structure is concerned, that's gigantic. This means that we really need, as parents, to try and structure everything in the house. There is a wake-up time, there is a bed-time and there is a scheduled dinnertime, so they know what to expect. If you tell them something, be true to your word. Don't say that you're going to do something and then not do it. It starts from what time you're going to eat, to who is going grocery shopping so that they can make their meals, all the way through to "You know we are going to do this.... as a family this weekend." This is so important as a parent, to keep structure for these guys.

Christina: Just to touch on two more things my mom said. The drinking—as you're in your early twenties or even early thirties—I hope other people listen to this: alcohol is a drug. It's a legal one, but it's still a drug, and it alters your brain. As someone who has a bipolar disorder, you should know that this will have an extreme effect on you.

Don't over drink and don't drink hard liquor. That's about the best advice I can give you. I tried to test this out myself and it was awful. I really do monitor how much alcohol I consume, whether it is a couple of beers or two glasses of wine: I have my limit and I try to stay within it.

The other thing I wanted to talk about is being organized, which goes along with structure. Keep your room clean and orderly. I know my Mom and I battle about this a lot. I've been working really long hours right now, so it's been hard to keep it clean. But, the cleaner the space you have, the cleaner mind you will have. Less anxiety. Less stress. Just put everything away where it goes and then you don't have to stress about it or be overwhelmed over a messy room. Put things away as you go. Putting things away as you use them in the kitchen is an easier route than having to deal with a big messy kitchen. There are a lot of ways to avoid that trigger by keeping everything in its place.

Angela: Once again, you know I understand how courageous this is and how much courage it takes to be this raw and honest about everything. I really appreciate it Christina, thank you.

I found something on Facebook the other day and it's from Bring Change 2 Mind. This is the organization that was started by Glenn Close and her sister, who is bipolar. And the sister has a son that is not only bipolar but also schizophrenic. I can't really remember what the name of that particular diagnosis is, but Glenn Close started this organization that really seems to be catching some great traction.

I wanted to leave you with the quote from there but I also want to encourage you to find them on Facebook and follow them. They are not just for bipolar disorder but for all mental illness. They are generally trying to stop the stigma of mental illness, and I think they are fantastic. So this is from Bring Change 2 Mind: "When you find someone isolating perhaps yourself, reach out, share your story, listen without judgment, ask for help, connect with empathy and compassion. Stay afloat with the BC2M which is the Bring Change 2 Mind Community and let's have a stigma free summer."

Christina: You are never a victim, but forever a fighter.

Additional Resources

Angela and her guests have put together a collection of resources to help parents of challenging children. It includes nutrition and exercise advice, checklists and other useful tips and information.

You can get a copy by visiting

http://www.dftok.com/bonus-page

What I Gained From Losing Everything

This chapter discusses the tragic loss of Jacquie's daughter and how this affected her and her family's life. Jacquie's story pulls on everyone's heart strings while she reveals her motivations for helping others and gives an honest critique of society's lack of effort towards helping those with mental illness and addiction.

Jacquie Tyas works as a mental health youth justice social worker. She is also the mother of two adult children. Her oldest son, who is now twenty-seven, has struggled with mental health issues for most of his life. His formal diagnosis was Tourette Syndrome, Attention Deficit Hyperactivity Disorder (ADHD), Learning Disorders (LDs), Obsessive Compulsive Disorder (OCD) and rage disorder. He has struggled since his teens and continues to, with serious addiction issues.

Jacquie is a Program Supervisor at Turning Point Youth Services, which is a multi-service accredited, children's mental health centre. They are located in Toronto's downtown core and provide a range of mental health, counselling and support services, to at-risk and vulnerable youth aged twelve to twenty-four years old and their families.

This interview was first recorded August, 2013.

Angela: I am sitting in a secret location somewhere in the Greater Toronto Area, in Ontario, Canada with my guest Jacquie.

Jacquie: Hi there!

Angela: One of the best parts of my newfound second profession is that I get to interview my favourite people. Jacquie is one of the most inspiring people I have ever met in my life; she's gone through some of the most horrific circumstances and has come out not just surviving and not just thriving, but giving back to the world in a profound way. She took pain and transformed it into a powerhouse of healing, and is conquering working in the healing industry now, dealing with her issues. All this being said, let us learn more about Jacquie and what it took for her to be where she is today. Hopefully everyone out there will find her story relatable and learn something new that could help them with their own life struggles.

So, Jacquie, welcome!

Jacquie: Thank you. Where my life really took a turn was about twenty-five years ago. The potential for all of us to be able to move forward even with severe challenges and tragedy is totally possible for everyone. I am proof.

It was 1998. I was coming home from a drive-in with my newborn son, my teenage daughter and my husband at the time. We were hit head-on by a drunk driver. I was very seriously injured, my newborn baby received a head injury, my husband at the time had a substantial head injury and my daughter died.

Prior to that, life had been pretty good and I hadn't been challenged in any great way; certainly nothing like this. Over probably the next five years I did not think I would be able to survive. It was the pain: it was just absolutely unbearable. I did have a support system but I certainly could not be comforted. Nobody I knew had experience with what I was feeling. Though many tried, they could not possibly grasp my heartache. I was isolated. There were times I actually contemplated suicide because I didn't think it would be possible for me to move forward without my daughter in my life. The pain was unbearable. I had never experienced that kind of pain. It was overwhelming, both emotionally and physically.

After a while, I realized that I had to be strong, if not for myself then for my son. I knew I did not want this tragic event to be my or my son's legacy. It was then that I decided I had to move forward. This was a defining moment for me. Deciding to move forward helped motivate me to devise a plan.

I had been in bed for about three months that year. I'd lost a considerable amount of weight. I wasn't eating and could not imagine how I could live without my daughter or live with never seeing her again. I had made a decision that if I couldn't find someone that had survived tragedy and was actually living their life in what I consider to be normal and with some purpose, then I was going to take my life.

I remember when I was in the hospital, I was given a pamphlet from family services, they said "call us if you ever need us" but I didn't; I didn't really feel that it was necessary. Those days there just wasn't really any other choice. I decided to call them and if someone could give me proof that they survived, then I would reconsider my plan of suicide.

Fortunately enough, a wonderful woman who doesn't even know that she saved my life that day, spoke to me and was very supportive. She was able to laugh; was able to talk about her life and the things that she was doing. She seemed to have found a new purpose even after the death of two children. I got off the phone and I thought, "if she can do it, I can do it." I didn't know what it was going to look like, but the one thing that I realized at that point is that I wasn't alone.

I then joined a support group with other mothers. Even though it was a very small group, they had experienced the same circumstances; their child had been killed and had dealt with a lot of pain and tragedy. Even though it was still very difficult, I started to realize that I wasn't alone. This did happen to other people, and there could be a new purpose in life. I wasn't exactly sure what that was going to be at the time. I also felt I could not make that my infant son's legacy, who also suffered a head injury. He needed me. I knew the pain I was in and I couldn't willingly inflict my pain or suffering on my child.

It was at that point that I started to figure out what my purpose was going to be. I decided to go back to school. I'd always thought of service and being involved in social work. The one thing that I realized as I started to heal (which took a very long time), is that I wouldn't have survived without the support of people who accepted me for where I was and were able to just listen and help me with my own pain. I knew at that point, that would be my purpose. I would try and provide the same sort of support that had been given to me in my healing process. It wasn't one particular person; it was a lot of people that genuinely cared and weren't afraid to hear what I had to say. It was terrible and painful, and they were willing to bear witness to my thoughts, accept me for where I was, and not make me feel that there was something wrong with me.

Angela: I remember when I met you, Jacquie, you were originally talking about getting involved in victim services?

Jacquie: Right.

Angela: And what made you switch, from victim services into social work and helping kids with mental illness?

Jacquie: The reason that I made that switch was my son. At five or six years of age, he started to really struggle emotionally and socially; he was having difficulty being happy. He started to do some really unusual things that I didn't understand. It took quite some time and a lot of advocating to even understand some of the things that he was going through. It was then that I experienced the lack of services, the lack of understanding, empathy and practical resources for parents and children. A young person with mental health issues requires resources. Their behaviour is just symptomatic of their inability to develop proper strategies to help themselves. It was because of this lack of servicing and understanding as a parent—the pain and the disappointment of wanting something more—that I felt that I would be better serving young people with complex mental health issues and their families. And that's when I decided that I would get into social work.

As my son became an adolescent he started to really struggle. He started using drugs, was very impulsive and had to be monitored at all times. He was violent, unable to control himself, on major medications and was monitored weekly by a psychiatrist and a whole lot of other service providers. There was just not enough servicing to support him, or any real understanding of what his needs were, and as a parent it was really difficult because there wasn't any other parent that I could talk to. I remember getting the initial diagnosis, which was Tourette Syndrome, but there were a multitude of diagnoses: OCD, ADHD, acquired brain injury, learning disabilities… It was great to get that diagnosis, but I remember saying to a friend, "Well that's great, but I don't know how to parent this person, and what do I do? It doesn't change anything other than now we have a name for it. It doesn't change anything."

I realized how at risk young people—particularly adolescents—were being arrested and put in the criminal justice system because of their mental health issues. As a program manager for a youth justice detention facility for young men, my approximation is that eighty-five percent to ninety percent of them have mental health issues that have not been diagnosed, or they have not been supported. They're being arrested based on their inability to function in the environment that they're in. Every young person with mental health issues has trauma. That trauma in itself creates even more complicated mental health issues on top of the diagnosis or the initial mental health issue.

They then become further and regularly traumatized by teachers that don't understand, schools that aren't prepared to support them and create programming that is appropriate for them; parents not having any supports, parents not having anybody to talk to; or anybody that's really willing to understand or not blame them. On top of that, parents are traumatized, children are traumatized and that creates a comorbidity of mental health issues which create even further problems and often lead to suicide. Once that diagnosis has been made and depending on what it is, medications and good psychiatric support, and family counselling support can be effective and are lacking in our system.

It's the world at large that creates this stigma and, you know, we're getting better, but it's very subtle. What it says to the parent, and what it says to the young person with mental health issues is, "There's something wrong with you and you don't fit in the world," and that translates into, "I don't have a place in the world and I'm worthless, and regardless of what I have to offer I will always be blamed for something that is not within my control…" That feeds into desperation. That is repeated; more and more trauma is inflicted on a young person; and then of course, on the parents. As a parent, what I know only too well is the agony of knowing that your child doesn't fit in. Other people are insensitive to it, and the young person is being bullied on a regular basis. Bullying is sometimes emotional, and sometimes physical. Sometimes there is just complete detachment which again translates into, "I am nothing and I am invisible."

For me, doing the work that I do is because of my own child, who has probably been in every psychiatric facility that there is—long term and otherwise. Having to advocate for him was physically and emotionally exhausting for me. Then, as he became an adult, being traumatized myself, by watching him spiral into drug abuse and not being able to help control it anymore, was agonizing. What was worse was not having anybody to assist me. Unfortunately, addiction and mental health go hand in hand; not always, but there is a higher risk of young people turning to drugs to cope, and when these are combined with psychiatric medications it can be a deadly mix. The reality is, young people end up being criminalized for their mental health issue. As a parent having to see your child—who is vulnerable—living on the streets, and knowing that you can't help them because there are not enough support systems, is just wrong. We need to have a clear understanding that every young person who comes into custody requires extensive support services, and any young person with mental health issues requires support from their community at large.

Angela: How are you feeling about the support services system for parents dealing with these kids, either incarcerated or who have been in these situations? Do the parents really understand that their children in most cases suffer from some kind of mental illness? Are you able help in setting them up with social services? If the parents do not know, are they supportive of the help? How are they reacting when you try and get these things in-gear for them?

Jacquie: Well I have to say that the agency that I work for is unique because we are the designated mental health agency for youth that come into a detention setting. This is a good thing generally, because detention is a punitive approach, not a treatment approach. This is why I work for the agency that I work for. I am committed to, and believe in the values and the missions of the agency. We believe that most young people are suffering from mental issues when they come into custody, and that's how they ended up there. They are immediately assessed by a forensic psychiatrist and we do a full assessment to determine what they need.

We are a one-stop agency, so if the youth is in our custody there is access to clinicians, family counseling, anger management treatment, substance abuse treatment, psychiatric care and medication prescribed by the forensic psychiatrist, who is a specialist and works strictly with youth and with complex mental health issues. We are unique. If the youth is to leave our care, we have appropriate housing and supports available to those who are in need. Usually aftercare is something that is generally very limited. There are huge waiting lists, and it doesn't meet the needs of the young person.

The minute someone comes into our care, we have transitional workers who meet with them right away to start looking at their plans for housing and plans for support afterwards. Whether they're going to go to school or work, our people act as advocates for that young person. Our role is to assist them with the challenges that they experience on an ongoing basis. We want to ensure that they're able to come back into the community with appropriate supports, so they don't keep getting rearrested, and that they're able to be successful in the community and receive support for their mental health issues.

Angela: It sounds sadly a lot like my daughter's experience. Sadly, it's not OK when one of the greatest things that could happen to a person is trying to kill themselves, so they can be hospitalized in a residential treatment facility. If getting arrested is the greatest thing that can happen, so they can come under your care… since when is either one of those things a lucky break?

Our system only works under the most horrible of circumstances. One of the frustrations that you have had is being on both sides of the system. How are you feeling about the resources that are in place for parents and child? When do they know they need help? There are a lot of parents out there who need help. But it is difficult— almost impossible. It's really hard to get anything in place.

Jacquie: There are crisis facilities where things happen on an intervening basis, but as far as prevention goes there is still not a lot out there. We've come a long way as far as the stigma of mental health, but I think schools have to come a lot further from where they are. There are a lot of boards of education who are not willing to look at things until they become a huge issue. There are some boards that are better than others and I will talk about which ones—in Toronto—because it is so diverse.

There are so many people—young people—in crisis, there are early intervention programs within the school setting. They are three year programs, for a young person who is just going into school and starting to exhibit signs of mental health challenges and that requires extensive supports. They are few and far between, and sometimes it takes years to get them into these programs. Funding has been cut, which is the big issue, so they don't have proper funding to help.

Until there is a crisis and they have to deal with it, it goes on a hierarchy of the most needed, regardless of all the young people who need it. Even in our government's Ministry of Health funding, there isn't enough to provide for preventative tactics. There needs to be a focus on intervention based on varying degrees of crisis. This is the reason we have mental health safe beds for a person that's homeless and in crisis. It's a temporary measure that gives a person with mental health challenges only thirty days of safety off the streets. There are hospitalizations if you're in crisis. You can go to the hospital, but whether they will actually admit you into the hospital is dependent on a lot of factors. Unfortunately most people that have mental health challenges cannot can be put under Form 1 by a medical doctor.

Angela: Tell me what Form 1 is for people who don't know what it is.

Jacquie: Form 1 is: you are in a state of crisis and you are not able to make decisions for yourself because of some sort of mental health crisis. You are a threat to yourself or somebody else. A doctor will, in fact, issue it in these circumstances, and it allows for you to be detained for seventy-two hours in a hospital setting for psychiatric observation.

Angela: Any last remarks on this for everyone out there?

Jacquie: We need to intervene at a young age, and I think it starts at the educational level. That's the place where the young people spend seventy-five percent of their young years. The world has progressed, so have the needs of our society. There need to be changes made to provide up-to-date education on proper tactics and methods that are real and reliable for our educators. Hiding our children from the real issues only impedes their survival. School is where it's most evident, when they start to struggle emotionally and socially, and the supports are needed at that point.

The Canadian Mental Health Association is starting to develop what's called early intervention programs for young people, to prevent early psychosis that may be avoidable if the supports are there. Young people can be quite manageable, and not go on to develop full blown schizophrenia or psychosis, if there is intervention through medications, treatment and clinical observation.

Angela: OK Jac, you are, as always, an amazing person to speak to for the pulse on mental health today. It is an exceptional opportunity that you're here. I really appreciate that, and I thank you for your thoughts. We're just going to wrap it up for now. Next week, maybe you could tell us a little bit more about your son and how that all evolved. I know that you did some work in advocating with him to the school system. If we could talk a little bit further about that, it would be great.

A Quick Favour…

If you're enjoying reading this book, please review it on Amazon. The more reviews a book has, the more Amazon promotes it, which helps more parents find it. Also, if you haven't subscribed to the podcast on iTunes yet, please do—and leave a review there too.

Every little bit helps.

Tough Love

In this chapter, we continue our talk with Jacquie about the hardships she faced, and continues to face, with her son and his mental illness. Jacquie expresses many of the issues she encountered with different support systems, and offers some great advice from a well-informed perspective.

This interview was first recorded September, 2013.

Angela: We are back with Jacquie, and I just wanted to give a little intro. Jacquie is an amazing human being; one of the greatest people I have ever known in my life. She has been to hell and back in her life and has done great things, in spite of her struggles. We are here talking about her truly unique experiences when dealing with different kinds of mental illness. Today we will talk, parent-to-parent, about her experiences with her son. Hopefully, this will make you out there feel less isolated as a parent. Without further ado, here is Miss Jacquie!

Jacquie: I'll start off talking about my son, who is now twenty-seven, and as we said before, there weren't a lot of supports available. I spent most of his young years advocating for him within the school system, and actually trying to find people who could find out what was wrong with him. He was eventually diagnosed with

Tourette Syndrome. At that time, we started to see a doctor at the clinic for Tourette's, where he was also diagnosed with ADHD and OCD. All of these were caused by a head injury from the car accident when he was an infant. At the time we had no information on how that would affect his mental health as an adult.

Angela: Can I ask you to describe what your son's behaviour was like, in terms of actions and how he presented himself?

Jacquie: From about the time he was three years old onwards, I always noticed he seemed a little bit different in the way that he socialized. His responses emotionally were always very extreme and not appropriate to the disappointment of a three year old. He had an inability to stay still for any length of time, was very clumsy, unhappy, often crying and feeling frustrated. For example, music frustrated him. He just seemed to be always in a state of agitation.

I started to notice that he wasn't able to socialize with others his own age. When he was very little it wasn't really that noticeable, but when he got to about age six, it started to become more apparent. He just didn't know how to socialize; he didn't really read others' cues well. He was in his own world, just consistently having clumsy accidents and acting extremely out of control.

Angela: Yes, I remember very well my daughter Christina at those ages, and it's not that they're the same at all, but they're similar in their actions. We used to call her the 'drama queen'. Her behavior was centred around, "Oh my God, the world has ended because this small thing happened." It seems to be common among kids who have an undiagnosed mental illness.

Jacquie: For his chronological age, he didn't have the ability to self-regulate at all. He would act like an untrained child, and those without any understanding would think he was just spoiled and that no limits were set on him. Generally, everything was difficult for him.

In Grade 1, he had a very intolerant teacher who really didn't understand him. He was bullied in the school yard. He went for day care in the same school, and he would not be able to get from his classroom to his day care room without someone assisting him. If not, there would be no coat, no boots: there would be none of the things he needed to go home. He had to be watched very closely because he was known to act impulsively—worse than other kids his age.

I was worried that something was seriously wrong especially when he began wake up in the middle of the night crying and wouldn't be able to stop. It got to that point where I was always afraid for him to fall asleep, because if he woke up he would be crying for an hour.

Angela: Do you think the crying was caused by night terrors?

Jacquie: I think it was night terrors, but I also think it was just emotional dysregulation and inability to control his emotions on any level. There were odd things happening at the same time. I remember a teacher in Grade 2 had brought to my attention that his language was very advanced for his age, very sophisticated: he was discussing gargoyles. Generally a kid in Grade 2 has no idea what a gargoyle is, and what it represents. He grasped a lot that the other children didn't.

He was very high functioning in specific areas—like a savant—but then in other areas he was slow, specifically in social and emotional development. The social and emotional areas caused him a great deal of pain and uncertainty. He had to be supervised at all times. He just couldn't manage at all.

That became a real challenge. He was able to verbalize very well but couldn't read anything, even though he was read to every night and he memorized books. It wasn't until I missed a page and went to another, and he recited the page, that I realized he couldn't read. It was at that time that we sent him to a psychologist for testing. All the concerns I had were validated and he spent probably two years (from ages eight to ten), seeing a psychologist in private sessions to teach him how to read. He became very good at reading, but then other issues started to arise.

Sensory problems became prevalent. He couldn't listen to a lot of music; couldn't tolerate the sensation of certain fabrics on his skin; by the time he was eleven or twelve years old, he wouldn't leave my side; he would rather wet himself than go to the bathroom by himself; I always had to tuck him in the exact same way every single night before he could settle.

Then, he started to be terrified of being alone. He became a prisoner of his own body and mind. It was really quite frightening. He was then diagnosed with Obsessive Compulsive Disorder.

Angela: And that was about what time?

Jacquie: He was about age eleven. Things continued to get progressively worse. As he got older, the social and emotional differences between him and his peers became really evident. As a result, he was bullied really badly. Teachers were insensitive to the bullying. This destroyed his 'soul'. I think all parents of children with mental health issues can relate. The only thing we don't want them to do, is give up.

Their recovery begins with forming a new sense of identity. However, when they are constantly in recovery, it begins to take a toll on their ambitiousness and risk-taking. These are both necessary for their growth. They need to be able to take risks and be fearful.

The destroying of a young person's 'soul': that's pretty much what happened. The succession of bullying, inappropriate school programs, teachers that were totally insensitive and refused to try—despite psychological assessments and letters from doctors explaining the circumstances... There has to be a willingness.

The most painful memory was him moving to a new school in Grade 5, and knowing it wouldn't go smoothly. On the first day of school I was told that there was no full-time assistant to help him stay out of harm's way, and I just would have to wait until they got one.

The school did eventually get an assistant but they didn't really understand his needs. Two months into the program, he was hiding in the bathroom stalls at recess, crying. It was just agonizing, as a parent, to know that he would sneak into the bathrooms so that he wouldn't have to go out into the schoolyard. The school wasn't even sensitive to that, and of course then it got progressively worse.

All of the situations had the same undertones, which spoke to his inability to read social cues that made him vulnerable and that made him easily victimized. As a young person he never fitted in; he was always the kid that was never picked for group activities. Teachers at his school allowed for children to be excluded from groups, which only made it worse.

At twelve or thirteen years old, there were times he came home from school crying, not understanding why he didn't have any friends or why people were so mean to him.

When he got to high school, the kids had matured by then and there was less bullying. Sadly, he got involved in drugs to fit in and found friends through drug use.

Angela: It also probably gave him a way out: that ability to numb the mind to the point where the pain can be silenced.

Jacquie: Yes, exactly. Drugs made him feel good, gave him friends, and he didn't have to deal with the terrible obsessive compulsion, anxiety and trauma caused by years of bullying. At age eighteen he refused to take all of his medications. He started to get very heavily into methamphetamine drugs by injection. Within a short period of time was highly addicted, living on the streets, violent, not on any psychiatric medications.

Over the last ten years, he has basically lived in that state. He has been sober in between for very short periods of time and lives the life of a chronically homeless, mentally ill addict, with very little supports available to him. When I say supports available to him, I mean ones that are effective for people with mental health challenges and addictions, who are chronically homeless. There is not a lot out there to meet their needs. It's very difficult as a parent: you can't become part of that life. You can't get caught up in it because it doesn't help anybody. The only supports available are if you've been arrested, or if you are in a state of crisis and need hospitalization.

The fact he hasn't killed himself is surprising, but the fact is, he is killing himself. This is just active suicide portraying a state of daily life, rather than committing one final act. I think that as a parent, and particularly as a social worker, it's really difficult to accept the fact that you can't help your own child. And it's not shameful, but it is agonizing. It's very difficult to live your day-to-day life. You have to be able to separate your existing life, knowing that you'll have to watch your child self-sabotage and slowly kill themselves. The hardest of all is knowing that you are not able to assist them or intervene in any way that can help them.

Angela: I know there's a lot of debate over how much parents can know about their children's health and mental health after the age of eighteen, but it probably starts around sixteen? Would you agree?

Jacquie: Yes, it's actually sixteen. Basically, any young person under the age of sixteen can be helped with proper intervention and supports, but if you are aged sixteen and you're in family crisis, they will not intervene. That applies for a young person that is arrested and comes into care. Under the Youth Justice Act, parents are to be informed up to the age of eighteen but a youth has to give consent after the age of sixteen to allow their parents to be a part of their case management planning and to be advised of any of their medical information. That is entirely the choice of the child.

Angela: So did you get ousted from his life around the age sixteen?

Jacquie: Well, up until he was eighteen and because he really knew how out of control he was, he always allowed me to be an advocate on his behalf. To the point where at twenty-six years old he would like me to still do it, as if he was a small child, but I can't do that. It's against the law, not to mention that service providers will not allow the parent to be the voice for the young person.

Angela: That's tough.

Jacquie: Yes, it is very tough.

Angela: He's not in the right mind to be making decisions. It's not like he actually has the ability or the capacity to connect these dots, right? So that's very difficult.

Jacquie: That's where it becomes really challenging for most parents. Their young adult children have become addicted to a substance, have become involved with the criminal justice system, and require psychiatric help. Most doctors won't do it because patient advocate lawyers will have them released if the person doesn't want to be there. The law clearly states that unless you're a threat directly to yourself or someone else, you cannot be held against your will and you cannot be forced into treatment. And that's a good thing, but ultimately it doesn't help for intervention. You might be harming yourself and doing a lot of things that are very unhealthy, but unless you're at risk, in the moment of suicide, or in the moment of committing homicide or assault of another person, then it doesn't apply.

It's sort of a standard awareness between people in community service work that if a mentally ill person with a serious addiction comes into their hospital, he will be released. They do not want to deal with long-term rehabilitation necessary for a heroin addict or a methamphetamine addict who requires detoxification, medical treatment and a medical detox, intense therapy and then stabilization of the mental health, before they can deal with the addiction. The medical system refuses to care about the people who clearly need it the most. People need proper care not just Band-Aid solutions.

Angela: That's really difficult. I would like to end every interview with something that's at least a bit positive. If you were going to give advice to a parent of a mentally ill young adult, how would you go about doing that, whether they're drug addicted or not?

Jacquie: My son is in a state of constant crisis, and is actually violent because of addiction, mental health issues and active psychosis. I cannot be physically around him because it's dangerous, but there is some connection. My son knows how to get hold of me when he wants to talk to me. Even though I find it shocking and emotionally overwhelming, he needs to be given the consistent message that, "I will be here." You need to detach from them, but consistently send out that same message: "I'll be there for you, and I love you no matter what's going on." Listening to the hard things about their lifestyle as a result of their mental health and addiction issues is really hard. I think that would be the advice I would give: that even though you think your kids won't hear that, they do hear it and they do know that you love them even if you're not helping them or supporting them. That's huge.

(Angela and Jacquie begin to giggle.)

Angela: OK Jacquie thank you so much. I really appreciate that you were here today to share that with us. Forgive Jacquie and I for giggling, we are known to have an inappropriate sense of humor in the best of times. I think that it comes with the territory. We can be totally inappropriate.

Jacquie: I was going to say that's emotional instability from parents that are just exhausted and tired. If you don't laugh, you'll cry. It's pretty much that. I think for parents out there that are dealing with constant stress, laughing can provide you with some emotional instability at times. Hysterical laughing is actually a relief, as crazy as that sounds. I think that most parents in our circumstances at some point have laughed at things when it was totally inappropriate to be laughing at them, it's our own form of stress relief.

Angela: It's also that it's just so unreal. It's so ridiculously out of the realm of what anybody else would experience that it does strike me as funny. It is like a Saturday Night Live episode that goes on in my head all the time. I have now developed a very offbeat sense of humour, the results of which we deal with day in, day out.

Jacquie: Right. It's a coping mechanism. It can be overwhelming dealing with these struggles and often really bad situations.

Angela: You have an offbeat sense of humour and you are the parent of a child that is mentally ill. You are in great company. This is one of the many ways in which we cope. It's probably the most positive way, just to be able to laugh about the bad and try to remember the good.

Dealing With Intolerance And How I Got Through It

Jacquie opens up about the trouble her son had in the education system. She and Angela provide a deeper look at the emotions and mental strength it takes to care for a child with a mental illness. As well, they share some advice on how approach a school system that is failing to support your child.

This interview was first recorded September, 2013.

Angela: How different is our reality from other parents? My daughter's actions were overblown at times, and other parents would look at me with judgment as if to say, "Can you get your kid under control? She's really losing it over nothing." I would like to talk to Jacquie about these types of situations and get her perspective on things. Her son encountered a lot of stigma associated with mental illness. Jacquie, thank you very much for coming.

Jacquie: I would say much of my parenting experience dealt with being isolated from others because of parents not understanding my situation. People would make their judgments—some subtle and some direct—such as Angie mentioned, saying things like "Get your kid under control." This resulted in exclusion by the other parents. There was never an invitation to events or group participation.

Then, of course, you have the feeling of being inadequate as a parent, thinking, "Oh well, what can I do to be more accepted in this group while my reality is very different?"

I have a lot of stories of bad treatment of my son, but first I want to share a good one. We went to my son's kindergarten 'teacher night' and there was an aquarium filled with fish. All the kids were playing and I was talking to the teacher and keeping an eye on my kid. When I got home that night he was undressing and all the fish fell out of his pockets. He did say how much he liked those fish, but I never gave it any thought, nor did I see his hands going and collecting them and neither did anybody else.

This kindergarten teacher was a very special lady. We decided that we would just replenish the fish tank, and the teacher never mentioned what had transpired. We just received a nice thank you card that all the kids and the teacher had made, thanking us for the fish. That was a teacher that really understood. She took a very unusual situation, and was able to turn it around and turn it into a positive thing.

Other circumstances have been absolutely agonizing for my son, and for me as a parent to watch. I remember when my son went into Beavers, which is supposed to be about building self-esteem and an opportunity to socialize with young men through mentoring. His inability to sit still or participate fully was a challenge. The leader called me up to say they didn't want him to go anymore. I offered to have a personal support worker go with him, so he could be assisted if he was disruptive, but they said 'no'.

Angela: Did you ever find out why? I would assume that you had some backlash from parents during that period of time. Do you think there was some parental pressure?

Jacquie: Yes, there was. Many parents just didn't want their kid around my kid. They were mean spirited and didn't have any understanding or tolerance. They didn't want their children and their community activities being subject to a young person with unique behaviors.

Angela: Were his behaviors at that time violent or physical?

Jacquie: They were not violent at all. I think the violence, to be honest, occurred after years and years of bullying and abuse. He had feelings of rage later on because nobody wanted to associate with, or include, someone who embodies difference.

He was disruptive in the sense that he was loud. At school, he was disruptive to the program and needed to be removed from time to time just because he'd be so over excited, and ridiculously silly, which was disruptive. Even though I said, "Look, I will get someone who will actually help, then when he needs to be removed for a time out so that the rest of the group isn't disrupted, you can carry on," that was not acceptable to them. The parents didn't want that. That also happened when he was in hockey. Despite offering all those services, they actually refused him. It was just really heartbreaking to watch your child be hurt. Many people who have children who are bullied or excluded can relate to this awful, helpless feeling.

Angela: There must have been times when parents would have said something unkind to you or about you or about your son.

Unfortunately, I'm sure there are people listening that have had that experience.

Jacquie: I remember a specific situation, and it was absolutely astonishing to me, and so mean-spirited, that it still kind of traumatizes me. My son was playing with his brother. They were playing football, and there was an older boy who lived in the neighbourhood who was a bully by nature. He was physically assaulting my son; hurting him. My other son came back to tell me. I went to the family and explained to them that I was concerned about the beating my son took, and the parents basically turned it around on me. They said that it was my fault that my son behaved this way; that the kids needed to just be able to deal with it themselves, and that there was a problem with me and my kid, but not their son. They went on to say that if I knew how to be a parent then I wouldn't be dealing with this kind of nonsense. It was very difficult and I was absolutely astounded. I couldn't believe that even with the evidence in front of them, they refused to see. To them it wasn't an issue that their son was physically and mentally assaulting my son. To this day I still don't understand it.

Angela: That's totally traumatic. That is an awful story. Can you recount a couple of times in school, where your son wasn't welcome to participate when it was going to be a positive thing for him to have joined?

Jacquie: All of them happened when he was just going into Grade 8. He'd been struggling. He had had a personal educational assistant who wasn't very sensitive to his needs, was very punitive and was becoming a real problem. He was having more difficulty managing, but that was partly because of the challenges he was facing and partly from not being properly supported.

My son at that time started to smoking marijuana. He was at school and they found one marijuana joint on him. Obviously, he was suspended from school two or three days. But the awful part was, the school and the teachers refused to allow him to graduate and refused to allow him to participate in the graduation ceremony. This despite having several gains in the learning disabled classroom, and being integrated and really doing well. They refused to allow him to be part of the graduation ceremony, which is something he and I will never forget.

I'm still not really sure why the parents took such a stance against that. To me it was just extreme and mean-spirited, and it's one of those moments in your life when you see people and society for what they are. Society, and those within it, have a very low tolerance for abnormality or difference. That day they took away his chance to showcase his accomplishments, and instead made it about a mistake.

Drugs are a serious matter, but the reason why people seek drugs is much more important. If people were more sensitive to others' issues, all this negativity could have been utilized for a greater good instead of harm.

Angela: When you think about that now in retrospect—because that's many years ago now—is there anything that you would have done differently? Or is there any—for lack of a better term—advice that you might be able to give a parent in a situation like that?

Jacquie: I think I would not have accepted the principal's decision, which was driven by some of the parents who came forward and really didn't have any understanding of the circumstances. I would have advocated very strongly with the board of education and would have gone to the superintendent. I would have expected that he would be able to graduate with his peers. If supports were necessary, fine, but I would not have allowed them to take that away from him. I think at that time I was just so exhausted from the lack of support everywhere that I just didn't have the energy to try and explain my son's life to people who don't have a clue about what we go through.

Angela: That's the problem when you're going through all this. The parent is getting the challenging child mentally prepared for the event, speaking to the child to understand possible triggers and behaviours. It's the parent having to deal with their anxiety. So, by the time you actually get them to the event, you're always exhausted. If they are banned from participating, I bet you have no fight left.

We do everything we can to make it better, or a more auspicious occasion for them. I think it's a very common thing for a parent to feel mentally and physically 'run over'. Then you look back and say, "Maybe I could have advocated a little bit better," but you're a one-man band, and you did what you could at the time.

I know you did a lot of advocating. Is there anything that you can give as advice to a mother or father going into the school system, to advocate for their child? You are a social worker in the system now.

You might have a better look into how a parent might get the best results for their child.

Jacquie: I have learned a lot after years of advocating and having to spend a lot of money on lawyers and special services. The minute there is segregation, or any inappropriate behaviour or treatment of a child by students or peers, and if the principal is unwilling to rectify, seek solutions and put supports in place.

In the past I would probably have fifty meetings with the school. Today, if that happened, as soon as I found out about treatment that is inhumane or neglectful, I would get a special education lawyer and I would go immediately to the director of education. I would not put myself through that emotional turmoil ever again. You want to be cooperative and you want to develop a partnership with the people that are going to be in the school, but when you are not getting anywhere, you can't keep being at the mercy of them determining for you what is acceptable.

From Grade 5 'til about Grade 7, I spent a good portion of those two years in and out of the school. I would have to pick my son up from school every day because he was in so much turmoil. There were inappropriate supports and he was being harmed by the kids, quite seriously. I had to pull him out of school. I sought out a lawyer to deal with his right to an education; one that was safe. The minute that lawyer called the director of education, a meeting was set up and all of the things that my son required were given to him.

The appropriate professionals came in to explain to the school what the needs are because under the Education Act, every child is entitled to an education that meets their special needs. Once I got the 'no', I wouldn't try and fight the principal. I would be going directly to the administrator, and I would have a lawyer deal with that so I would not have to. It was far too emotional for me.

After years of spending a lot of money looking into private schools that I really couldn't afford, and home schooling options and everything in between, it was not until I hired a lawyer that I got help. I would suggest that once you've gotten that 'no', you take action. You take that action to the higher level, the director's level. I would have saved myself a lot of money and a lot of grief, and my child wouldn't have been so damaged.

Angela: Let's walk everybody through a meeting at the school. Well-meaning or not, it is an intimidating experience when you are in a meeting with multiple professionals for your child. I have come out of those meetings absolutely destroyed because I felt—whether it was their intention or not—that I was not heard. I was run over by whatever their directive was that day instead of putting something in place for my child.

Jacquie: I would totally support that, and I would say that I had many meetings like that in the early years. That was extremely difficult. My circumstances are a little bit different in the sense that in the first three years of my son's early education he had a wonderful program, a wonderful teacher and wonderful supporters, but then he moved out of that school board to being unsupported. I can tell you about one of the first meetings.

Angela: Who would be in the room?

Jacquie: The chief psychologist for the board of education, the principal, the vice-principal, the child and youth worker, and possibly the teacher. They worked to basically defend their position, downplaying the damage that was being caused to my son and justifying why they weren't meeting his needs. They tried to turn it around, as if the issue was with me and my parenting: I wasn't doing something right; what they were doing was right, even though it clearly wasn't working.

They totally ignored the reports that had been placed in front of them. I hadn't been heard. No matter how many times I told them what was going on with my son and the damage being caused, it was as if they didn't hear me. They just continued with the dialogue and their agenda. They talked about the special education plan, which was not meeting my child's needs and was damaging his emotional health, making him go into crisis and not allowing for him to be consistently at school because he was in an uncaring environment.

It was not until my son was left unsupervised at lunch time with kids that had serious conduct disorders that things changed. They were clearly aware that my son should never be left alone with his peers. He was vulnerable, and he was seriously assaulted. It wasn't until I removed him from school and sent a letter to the principal saying that I was not bringing him back to school under these circumstances, because he was unsafe, that they even began to respond.

Angela: I want to speak a little bit about the time, the amount of effort and the amount of exhaustion that a parent goes through in trying to care for and support a child with serious mental and emotional issues, and trying to work at the same time.

Jacquie: When he started going to see the psychologist to learn how to read, he used to go two or three times a week and my husband at the time would take him to those appointments. I was working for an insurance company and it was very stressful. I was not able to take lots of telephone calls, and not able to take lots of time off of work. About a year after, he was not able to manage at school at all. I had to be available at all times, because on any given day I could be called to pick him up because they couldn't manage him.

After nine months of working full time, I had to give up my job because he became my full-time job. I had to be available in the event that the school called me, which was often on a daily basis. Managing my son became a full-time job, and I would have never been able to work and provide that level of advocacy. It was also financially depleting because we had to look at special programming that was private in nature, to offset the servicing that he wasn't getting in school: the services that he should've been getting.

Angela: I feel very badly for the parents that are out there that are working full-time and trying to manage some of this stuff. It is extremely difficult.

I'm going to say good night to Jacquie and thank you so much for coming. You are always a pleasure to have and always a wealth of information.

The Power Of Art

In this chapter, we speak to an artist and a very inspiring individual, Danica. She works for Workman Arts in Toronto, where she is the membership manager and hospital liaison. She and many of her associates are creating positive changes in the area of mental health and addiction through art. The tagline of Workman Arts is 'Artists With Extraordinary Minds'.

Workman Arts has been around since the 1980s. It's a non-profit art organization that provides training and exhibition opportunities to artists that have received services for mental health and addiction.

This interview was first recorded August, 2013.

Consider this...

Elton John has an eating disorder. Paula Dean has panic attacks and agoraphobia, or used to at least. Emma Thompson and Brooke Shields suffer from depression.

What do Catherine Zeta Jones, Vivien Leigh, Mel Gibson, Jean Claude Van Damme, Margot Kidder, Sinead O'Connor, Linda Hamilton and John Pauley all have in common? They all have been diagnosed with bipolar disorder.

What I want to get across here is that mental illnesses are not a prison sentence. There are many people that wouldn't be the brilliant artists they are without their illness. Their contribution wouldn't exist without their challenge. I don't want to get too carried away with the link between creative genius and mental illness, but it does exist and should be recognized.

Angela: I should probably tell you guys how I met Danica. We're currently sitting on a boat in Toronto Harbour and the reason we're on location is because Danica lives here and I vacation here. Just about ten or twelve days ago, I went to an open mic night at the little bar that is here and this beautiful young girl gets up and knocks the heck out of Adele, Cee Lo and Aretha Franklin—it was amazing. Talented, with a beautiful voice, Danica owns the stage when she's on it.

When she got off stage, I thought I would ask for her card as you never know if there's a celebration that could be enhanced by somebody like Danica. So I took her card, then saw her the next night on stage with another band and she knocked the hell out of that too. Then on the Monday, I'd forgotten I already had her card when I found it again.

Looking at it, I was curious what Workman Arts 'meant'. It's interesting that just as I have been trying to get people to interview for this show who might be able to put a positive spin on things, Danica appears.

As Danica kindly agreed to be interviewed, I decided that I didn't want to take her away from where we are, here, as it's absolutely spectacular. Looking at the sky I would say that we're in for a beautiful night. We're sitting in the galley of my boat, and we're glad to have you guys along for the ride.

So, Danica, we have a little bit of a personal background on you, but can you tell me more? In particular, what is your professional background and how did you get involved in this organization?

Danica: My background is that I was born and raised in theatre. I was in my first show, *The King and I*, when I was aged five, and I played the littlest Siam child. Ever since then, I have been involved in community theatre. I went to an arts high school, and right out of high school I gained my first professional music theatre gig playing a nun in *Nunsense* in Petrolia, ON.

Since then I've been in a funk band called *The New Movement* for three years, and it has been a lot of fun. It gave me an introduction to song writing and how to sing for myself. I got into a lot of jazz and blues, which made me want to collaborate as much as humanly possible.

Like any working performer in a big city, I worked in a café serving coffee for five years, until I got a call out of the blue from a great stage manager friend of mine named Tracy Lin Kan. Tracy asked me to audition for a show in Amsterdam which was opening in the following two weeks. I auditioned and was subsequently offered a part in the production.

As it turned out, it was Workman Arts that was producing the piece. So I went to Amsterdam, did the show, and was hired two days after I got back to Toronto for their annual *Rendezvous with Madness* film festival, on a six week contract. After that, I became the administrative assistant with Workman Arts, then the membership and training assistant at Workman Arts, and now I am the membership and training manager. I also manage the portfolios of theatre manager, music manager and literary arts manager. I have been with Workman Arts since September, 2010.

Angela: Tell us about some of the programs that Workman Arts runs.

Danica: We provide training and exhibition opportunities in all disciplines. We have media arts, literary arts, visual arts, music and theatre arts. We have two training seasons a year and we have approximately three hundred artists with us right now. Across the disciplines, we run training opportunities. We love anything that runs from what we class as training, to creational presentation, to education, where we will train artists who will then create. We will then find (or make) an opportunity, with a great venue to present at and, in turn, we hope it educates the general population on mental health and addiction, as well as how the arts benefit the life of anyone who is handling their mental health, which—let's be honest—who isn't?

Angela: That's absolutely true.

Danica: We work with a small staff. Small but mighty! We are a staff of artists, not a staff of social workers. We work with artists as artists. as peers. Whatever brings an artist to our door is our business. It's a yes or no question: "Do you now or have you ever received services for mental health or addiction?" We do not require that anyone disclose anything beyond that.

However, when you're an artist, you are a person who expresses, and you're going to create and express what is close to you. So a lot of my favorite artists create self-portraits, and a lot of what you do in the arts is a self-portrait, even if it's indirect. So a lot of the art that comes out, a lot of the discussions that are started within the classes or different projects, are centred on mental health and addiction. We carry out a lot of outreach to youth, such as projects in schools. Anything that we can make public we will go public with, to start or continue really meaningful, worthwhile conversations around mental health, addiction and the arts.

Angela: So how important would you say art is to those that suffer from a mental illness of any kind?

Danica: Everyone needs an outlet, especially people with mental illness. Sports, engineering, and the arts are all universal languages. You can go anywhere in the world, hum a Gershwin melody, and find someone who can identify it. It's something that transcends language, geography, age, gender, economic status. It doesn't matter where you come from or where you're going, the arts will speak to you in some way, shape or form. It's unifying. It brings us together. And if you are dealing with your mental health, you need to be brought to other people. You need that social connection. You need to know that you're not alone.

Everybody needs an outlet. You need something that you're good at. You need something that you can put energy into and almost more importantly get energy from. When you can see something full circle and reap those benefits, it's empowering. You have to have something that's empowering, especially for youth. Especially when you're going through the worst of your mental health crisis.

These can be lifelong struggles. I see people in many different stages. It could be somebody who was a professional artist, high ranking in their field, who has suffered a breakdown and hasn't been able to draw since. We would help them try to come out of that rut, to get them again reaping the benefits of their talents.

There are people who discover their arts practice while they're in hospital or during their mental health crisis. They will identify or begin to express through their arts practice. We want to continue that again so that they can keep their momentum. It's not a distraction, it's an outlet. It's something that you need. You need the energy that you put out to come back to you, and everyone needs something that they're good at to get that energy back.

Angela: OK, without using any names of course, can you give me a story of somebody who has greatly benefited from your program and explain how it helped with their recovery?

Danica: Absolutely. In fact, this artist has become one of my really good friends. We were just on a remount of a show together. She's incredibly talented, and suffers from a wide array of issues historically, currently, presently, and probably will continue to in the future. She came to us and we did a project together which started as a training program for wearable art in the fashion world.

We brought in an incredible instructor, Elaina Sony, who designed blank canvases for garments that artists could begin to work with. Through this project, this artist flourished. She created the most incredible garments and since then has found a way to take her paintings and turn them into other garments: bathing suits, pants, shirts, shawls, shorts, anything. She's turned it into a business. My cell phone cover is an iteration of her painting. And she's found a way to do this with zero overhead. There are companies out of the US that she sends her prints to, and it's all done on an on-demand basis. She doesn't have a store; she has some things in some boutique stores. Ultimately, she has created an entire enterprise out of original pieces of artwork that can be sold, bought, worn or gifted. She's also into jewellery now; she's really turned it into a full-fledged career.

Angela: And how is she doing?

Danica: She's doing great.

Angela: From the time she came to you, I can only imagine the transformation.

Danica: Yes, she suffered from what I now know as OCD. She didn't like leaving the house or being in social situations. She struggled with alcohol and a lot of self-medication, but through this she's gotten to collaborate with a ton of artists that she never would have been exposed to before. Collaboration is really key, especially with visual arts. It's easy to create in a bubble. As soon as you start collaborating and you share and you create, it can really change you: not just your arts practice, but as a person as well.

Angela: Can you think of one more example, if you don't mind? A person who has thrived within the environment of doing this, and it has helped their life.

Danica: I do the intake interviews for our artists, so they come to me first. Some people are quiet, and sometimes I get a life story. One of the cooler stories is that I had a gentleman come in who had drawn, yet not taken any drawing classes. He would pretty much put a mug in front of himself and study the shades and the shadows and the contours. He has a scientific background, so he would date and time-stamp all of his drawings. They were pretty much black and white, quite boring to be honest, or very academic. He was a scientist, and he would go into work every day, but it was very isolating work. He would sit down with a beaker, and make his notes. He just felt that it was wrong. He had a bit of a breakdown, but he was able to go to his employer and take a mental health leave of absence, which is becoming more and more available in the workplace.

Once he got in touch with himself, realizing that he was dealing with mental health in a different way than he had before, he became far more creative and started doing studies of colour—complete abstract pieces of colour.

He's just brought in a new body of work where he's working on a larger scale, and I mean real abstract pieces; real beautiful pieces. And it's all colour. He no longer time-stamps them, and there are no dates on them. He won't even write notes about where he was in his house when he was doing this drawing. And again, it's collaboration: he really opened up and started working with the other artists, working on group projects.

I mean, he's just the nicest human being ever. And the conversations that I have on a daily basis with any of our artists are incredible, but the conversations I've been able to have with him, and the awareness that he has from a scientific background, is fascinating. He's able to approach himself in a way that not many people can.

It's a level of honesty. Honesty is something that I get where I work, whether you like it or not, but it does keep you honest. You can't bullshit around somebody who is so open with you, so it's an incredible daily exercise of constant honesty.

Angela: I would like to get into some of the programs, and talk a little more about that. One of the things on your website that caught my attention right away was your film festival, so can you describe what kind of subject material is covered at the film festival?

Danica: Absolutely. So, it's the *Rendezvous with Madness Film Festival*. I believe that we are in our 22nd year of the film festival, and it runs during the second week of November every year. You can find out more information on the website, which is

http://rendezvouswithmadness.com

Or through the Workman Arts website itself, which is

http://www.workmanarts.com

We put out films from around the world. We like to do premieres, either Canadian premieres or international premieres, on anything to do with mental health or addiction. We've had some incredible programmes over the years. I've been a part of four film festivals now, and we had *Brothers and Sisters*. We always fly in as many film makers or actors as we can, and every film is followed by a panel discussion.

For the past three years, we've been partnering with the TIFF Bell Lightbox. We'll put all of our films up there. So we will have our film in a beautiful venue, then we'll have a panel discussion afterwards, which usually involves a mental health professional in the field that the film discusses. We'll have somebody with lived experience, and we'll have somebody on the artistic side. So either a film maker, an actor, a producer, the writer, etc., will come out and speak to that as well.

We've had some absolutely beautiful pieces, and because we're an arts organization, we don't want to show a boring, didactic, 'talking head' kind of film; we want something that raises the discussion in an artistic way. We also don't want to slap it in people's faces. Some of the films that we get to screen can be really heavy, but we don't want something that weighs somebody down when they walk out. We want something that will trigger a social conversation afterwards, something that will make somebody go out for a drink afterwards and keep that conversation going as opposed to, "Wow! That was a heavy film! Let's go and distract ourselves from this topic of conversation now."

We usually have between twenty and twenty-five film programs. We also do lots of different live performances as well. A couple of years ago we had a program called *Lens of Illusion,* which starred Dr Bruce Ballen, who is a psychologist at CAMH and is also an illusionist. He works by trying to describe or show examples of different mental health issues or addictions through illusions. So he would bring up audience volunteers and mess with them. Through magic illusions, or whatever you want to call it, he will show the effects of depression, of memory loss, of anxiety.

We also worked with Andy Moroe, who is a phenomenal Toronto artist that Workman Arts works with quite frequently, to do a visual video projection throughout his entire presentation. So through projections, through illusions, through music, through movement, we were able to provide a sixty minute original show depicting different mental health and addiction issues.

Then we threw a big party because, again, we like to keep it social. You can't make things too heavy; you have to make them accessible to the general public. What better way to bring people together than to throw a big party? We had *The Carnival of the Mind*, food carts and photo booths: everything we could do to keep the discussion going. You have to have an environment conducive to those kinds of discussions to make it worthwhile and to make it last beyond the program itself.

We also had a fantastic comedian, Big Daddy Taz, who also calls himself the Bipolar Buddha—look him up on YouTube; he's amazing. But again, humour is an accessibility tool, and it's also a coping mechanism. If we can talk about it and find the humour, it's just something that continues the dialogue and continues the conversation.

Angela: That's very cool. I'm really intrigued with the film festival. If you can, give me your top three films and just a little bit of a synopsis. Or just give me three examples of films that made an impression on you and what the subject material was about.

Danica: We had a great film, and if I could remember the name of it, I'd be very happy right now. It was a family film, a documentary, called *My Brother Carl*, I think—it will come to me. We showcased it last year during our film festival, and it will be in our archives of our listings online. But the entire family came in. It was about the writer of the documentary's brother, who suffered quite severely from schizophrenia and he was very much a recluse. He had cut himself off from society and from his family. The film is about a family's outreach to a family member, but they really went into the rest of the family's issues, as well, and the struggles that everyone goes through. So, although there was one person that was the main subject of the film, it was really about how the rest of the family came together: their own struggles, their own unity, how they reached out, how they got him back. It was really quite a touching film, but honestly, through most of these films, it's the panel discussions afterwards that gives you the most insight into how the film came to be, how it started, and what that journey was for them.

Sisters and Brothers was our opening film a few years ago, it was also really fantastic. That was starring Cory Monteith, who passed away recently. It was also starring Gabrielle Miller, the Canadian actress who was in *Corner Gas* for so long. The two of them were just fantastic and we had Cory as part of the panel discussion.

The whole thing was mainly about addictions, but something that we talk about a lot in mental health too is, of course, the stigma. There's a lot of it. There's a lot of bias against the mental health or addictions issue, whereas, if someone had cancer, they would receive different treatment—sympathy, or support. When someone has a mental health issue or an addiction—especially addiction—a lot of people assume that it's a choice, an option, something they could walk away from if they chose to; or if they just tried hard enough. And that's not true. It is a disease; it is psychological; it is a struggle, and it is a lifetime struggle. Once you're an alcoholic, you are always an alcoholic. You may not show symptoms. You may not have had a drink in years. But it's still something that you hold on to for the rest of your life, so there's an understanding that comes with it.

I feel like the word stigma is stigmatizing on its own. I feel like as soon as you say anti-stigma someone says, "Oh! What is there to be afraid of? Clearly I'm missing something." So even when we deal with youth, we try not to use the word. I feel like it's being used in too many campaigns, and it glosses over what the real issues are. The real issue is that we're just not talking about it in the correct light.

We also had a great program in the first year that I was there, back in 2010. Ron Hynes, The Man of A Thousand Songs, and we showed his film which was incredible. The lifestyle of a musician dealing with mental health and addictions and concurrent disorders can be extremely difficult to even diagnose and to keep in check. When he came, we had an incredible conversation with another psychologist at CAMH. They brought out the psychologist on a gurney in a white lab coat. The two of them sat and had an incredible conversation, and then we had the musician play all night. And it was such an incredible evening of celebration. If someone can have the self-awareness to create a film about their own journey in a positive way you want to celebrate that. Again, it's about putting energy into something and having it come back, and feeling something full circle and reaping the benefits of your struggles.

You have to bring something out of it, otherwise it's lost time, and a lot of what I see is reclaiming. A lot of our artists who go through the mental health system feel they've lost time; they may even feel that they've lost a piece of themselves. And putting it through their art—seeing something positive—you're reclaiming it. You're reclaiming your time, you're reclaiming yourself. So there are a lot of full circles that I see happen.

Again, you have to be aware. You have to be self-aware. You have to be aware of those around you, aware of what your triggers are, aware of your environment, and aware of what you, as a person, want to be. That's where I feel very lucky: I'm surrounded by a population of people who have a level of self-awareness that you don't get in a lot of places. They have figured out that they need their arts and their arts practice to be the healthy person they know they can be. Having those two things line up in a single place with several different people is very empowering for the artist and for the staff, and for anybody who is lucky enough to be in that environment.

Angela: How many people attended the film festival last year?

Danica: Last year was a benchmark year for us. When the film festival started, we were still on the grounds of CAMH in the old Joseph Workman theatre. It's a big round theatre on Queen Street, at the end of Ossington. Since the redevelopment, we've moved to an old church which used to be the Equity Theatre showcase space. It was a lovely theatre space. We had our festival there before we moved into TIFF. Once we hit TIFF, we hit movie-goers. We moved away from like-minded organizations as our target audiences, and we hit movie and theatre appreciators as a target audience. So it really grew last year. In the past, we would show a film, and we might only have had an audience of twenty or twenty-five people. Last year we sold out.

One film I really need to mention, which I can't believe it has escaped me until this point, is called *The Maze*. It's all about the works of William Kurelek, who is a famous Canadian painter. He's most known for his prairie landscapes, but he did spend some time in Bedlem in Europe and started creating these incredible pieces, almost Bosch-esque. One of them is called *The Maze*, and it is an insight of what he felt his brain looked like. If you Google *The Maze* by William Kurelek, you will look at tiny little portions of these paintings as complete other worlds. Absolutely incredible. His sons actually went out and searched for his old pieces of work. They pulled some of his visual pieces, animated them and put them to music. One of the pieces is basically an orchestra of pigs. They animated it and put it to music. We put it up several times, and every single time it sold out; we'd have to turn people away and find another way to present this film. So we've really hit a different audience of people who are art appreciators, new movie appreciators, theatre appreciators who understand or can appreciate these discussions on mental health and addictions. And again, our panel discussions are always extremely popular and very strong, and they're starting to bring out a much higher attendance. When we showed *The Maze*, we had a few audiences of about five hundred a-piece. So our audience numbers are growing significantly.

We also worked with a fantastic publicist, Joanne, of Planet Free Communications, who works so hard to get us coverage. The film festival has been around for twenty-two years and it's still growing! I have extremely high hopes for us in the future. Toronto was so saturated with film festivals and niche markets that it's tough to try to rise above the saturation of film that we have in the city. We're still trying to find where our target audience is, but certainly being with TIFF has opened it up to the general population. You also don't want to preach to the converted: if we're constantly going to like-minded organizations, they already know this stuff. This is what they do. So to try to reach the general population has kind of been our new goal.

We also have a program called *Rendezvous In The Classroom*, which takes the film festival into schools. We've taken films from the program into schools to have conversations with youth. We've moved more towards universities and colleges, especially trying to partner with places such as George Brown College: places that have reputable, really great art programs. We've struck such incredible partnerships with these education institutions that there is a significant increase in young artists coming to our organizations. Young artists who may be new to their illness and who are serious about their arts practice because this is what they already committed a great deal of their life to. They're really forcing us to 'up our game' and create real, creative professional development opportunities for artists who are ready to enter it as a career.

Angela: That is fantastic. What an amazing program, absolutely fantastic. Danica, thank you so much for joining us today. I think we're going to go through another interview with you after this one. I'm so happy that you're here; I really appreciate it. You're giving us a whole different perspective where parents may be able to channel some of that extra energy. It's a form of therapy for young people. Thank you so much everybody.

The Art Of Mental Illness

In this chapter our host Angela again interviews Danica Brown, a membership and training manager for Workman Arts. Danica, through Workman Arts, is helping create positive changes in the area of mental health and addiction through art.

Workman Arts is an organization that promotes arts within the mental health community. She explains how this organization can help artists who have received services for mental health or addiction, to develop and refine their art practice through various programs. They aim to promote a greater public understanding of mental illness and addiction through art.

This interview was first recorded August, 2013.

Vincent Van Gogh said, "I am unable to describe what the matter with me is; now and then there are horrible fits of anxiety, apparently without cause."

According to an article by William Lee Adams posted on CNN World, researchers have found that people working in creative fields, including dancers, photographers and authors, were 8% more likely to live with bipolar disorder. Writers were a staggering 121% more likely to suffer from the condition, and nearly 50% more likely to commit suicide than the general population. They also found that people in creative professions were more likely to have relatives with schizophrenia, bipolar disorder, anorexia and autism. The numbers are staggering.

Some people in history that have had a mental disorder: Charles Dickens, Tennessee Williams, Ernest Hemingway, Leo Tolstoy and Virginia Woolf. Now, I don't want to get carried away with the link between creative genius and mental illness, but I did want to bring it to your attention to know that people with mental illness are just like those without one. And people like Robin Williams, Jim Carrey and Jonathan Winters did amazing work with their mental illness. Their comic genius wouldn't have existed without the presence of their illness.

Angela: I'm sitting here once again with Danica. Lovely to see you Danica, thanks so much for coming and talking with me today. Danica works for Workman Arts, which is an organization that promotes arts within the mental health community.

I'm really excited about this because it's such a nice, lovely, positive, upbeat opportunity for us to have a conversation about mental illness when some of the interviews can be a little bit heavy. We are on location in the galley of a boat. I met Danica as a fellow boater at an open mic night where she knocked the heck out of a few songs. She's an amazing performer, has an amazing voice and that's how we got to meet.

I am a weekend warrior on the boat, but this week I'm taking a week's holiday. I thought this would be a perfect opportunity to speak to Danica one-on-one and take the opportunity to let you guys know what she's doing, and what the organization is doing. It really is an uplifting, positive and fantastic organization. So welcome, Danica! If you wouldn't mind, tell me a little bit about your organization.

Danica: So I work for the Workman Arts project of Toronto. Workman Arts has been around for about twenty-six or twenty-seven years now. It started off as a program at Canadian Addiction and Mental Health (CAMH) and was founded by Lisa Brown. Lisa was a psychiatric nurse at CAMH who found herself gravitating towards the artistic. She started a separate organization, with its own board of directors, and it has been thriving ever since. We have about three hundred artists in all disciplines. We work with media artists, visual artists, performing artists, musicians and literary artists. We also provide training and exhibition opportunities to any artist who has received services for mental health or addiction. We do work closely with CAMH, but we work with artists who've received services from anywhere.

Our age range right now is fifties to sixties, but in the past two or three years we've had a great increase in a younger demographic, which raises a lot of really interesting questions like, "Are youth more comfortable talking about mental health earlier on in their diagnosis?" "Are they having these conversations amongst their peers?" "Are there more places for youth to reach out and to find the support?"

Also, within the arts community, artists now are becoming more comfortable divulging or speaking about their own struggles which they're going through. And of course, within arts, who isn't completely mad? To be an artist, who doesn't self-medicate within certain circles? And these conversations come out constantly. We've had incredible symposiums, discussions, debates, etc. The debates get extremely heated about what comes first: the artist or the madness.

Angela: I've often wondered that myself, because there's no clear division; there is no start and there is no end; you really don't know. You mentioned the Centre for Addiction and Mental Health. I know that there is a link to their site from yours. What is the background between the organizations? Because I know CAMH in Toronto is absolutely outstanding, as far as having cutting edge programs of all different kinds of mental illness. What is the connection there?

Danica: We like to say that we're a proud partner and are proudly supported by CAMH. We receive some operating funds from them. We'll partner with them especially for co-presentations, with our film festival or any larger project that we're working on, but we get most of our funding from arts organizations such as the Ontario Arts Council, Toronto Arts Council, Canada Arts Council and Heritage Canada.

We write grants; it's always grants-writing season in our office. We're always looking for ways to raise funds. We also have some independent sponsors who would come on board for larger projects. It's easier to get project funding when you have something shiny and marketable and packaged with a nice little ball around it. It's harder to find operational grants that allow us to continue to do the work that we need to be doing, but CAMH has always been an incredible source of resources for us.

If we're having any panel discussions, we have at our fingertips a wide array of individuals who are the best of the best at what they do. There are some incredible psychologists that we've worked with, and of course the occupational therapists and the recreational therapists are the people we go to, to help promote our programs.

We are at a point right now where we do have a waiting list for artists wanting to join the organization. I am now at the point where I might get two to three calls a day from artists looking to join the program. We don't have the capacity to continue growing at the rate that is being asked of us, but it is also forcing us to make connections with other like-minded organizations to make sure that nobody gets declined.

There has to be somewhere for an artist to find an outlet, to find a community, to find a psychologically safe environment for them to create and do the work that they need to do. So through CAMH, one project that we're just wrapping up right now is called *Arts Café*. It's through Addiction Medicine Services. They received an internal grant to hire our senior artists to provide arts programming on the CAMH campus. This gives our senior artists teaching experience. If you're a teacher, you are a critical thinker and you're someone who's going to continue to grow in whatever you're endeavouring to do. Providing paid opportunities for our artists to teach in a community that they've come from is starting to be a model that we're really chasing after.

We also have a group of actors who are hired by CAMH education services to provide what are called standardized patient scenarios and sessions. They are paid well to go in and role play as different clients as part of clinical training. We're actually the only organization that offers actors who have been through the mental health system to go back and be a part of mental health clinical training. This can be anything from concurrent disorders, and they can be very specific. We have a single actor go and do four sessions and play anything from a seventeen year old girl to a sixty-five year old male. A single actor would participate in four to five sessions.

Some of these are face-to-face with clinicians or over Skype, and can be across Canada. We work with incredible people at CAMH who are working very hard to get this program up on its feet. We hope to be able to offer it to different hospitals, not just psychiatric hospitals: we've been working with many different paramedics, etc.

What's really fun, too, is that we've been offering improv class for, like, a million years. Improv is very popular, and we've been working with the incredibly talented, super amazing Kate Ashby. Everything she does is incredible. She's such a super human being and she'll take on a group of twenty of our actors and put them through *Improv Madness*. It's just incredible what they do. I've seen people who are afraid to start conversations say the most outlandish things in front of an audience. Improv is actually beginning to get integrated into clinical training so that clinicians have a way of troubleshooting and problem-solving any instance or situation that might come up.

The first thing you learn in improv is to never say "no." If something comes up, you say: "Yes, and?" And to never dismiss, to never discourage, to constantly keep a line of communication open and keep momentum going and keep that ball up in the air. So **Kate Ashby**, who we've been working with for I think thirteen or fourteen years now at our organization, has been brought into different conversations through CAMH to talk about starting a really pointed improv training for clinicians at CAMH and other hospitals.

Angela: What are the other opportunities for people to be employed through Workman Arts?

Danica: In a number of different ways. We have an incredible art sales and rental program on our website for visual arts. Organizations, companies and businesses can rent paintings and write it off as an operational cost. We have programs where they can rent a painting for six months. What happens nine times out of ten is they have it up for six months, they love it, and they buy it. Great! Or somebody sees it, and they buy it. So we have a great art rentals and sales program.

We also have our acting opportunities and we're growing in our media arts department.

Film is a tricky industry at the best of times. We struggle to keep all of our programs accessible to any artist. A lot of our artists are on ODSP (Ontario Disability Support Program), a sort of assisted living. We want to make sure that if we offer something, we have the equipment available. That's been a bit of a struggle with film and media arts. We have senior artists—and by senior, I mean someone who's been working in the field for a while. We'll employ them as instructors, as Workman Arts member instructors, and they're incredible because they know the community that they're working with.

We have a great group of musicians who get hired as musicians in the community. And in a lot of ways, I feel like an agent sometimes. Someone will call me and say, "OK, I got this great thing going on. Here's the kind of feel that we're looking for. Who would you suggest?" I might suggest a piano player, one of our violin players, and a clarinet player.

We have a couple of small ensembles. I ran a small ensemble class for a few seasons at the organization on how to work and collaborate with different musicians. Music is a special art form; you can't do it in a bubble. It's very hard to do everything on your own as a musician: collaboration is key. It gives you someone to have a conversation with about choosing a piece of music, how to rehearse, how you get along together etc.

When you deal with artists who receive services for mental health or addiction, you're throwing quite a few personalities in a room in some situations, and you need different ways to negotiate that and work with people. There's an incredible amount of understanding and patience that our artists have for themselves and for other artists that work within our organization. But we are constantly trying to provide professional development opportunities that will result in a viable career for our artists, and we do track any money that our artists get through the organization.

We also try to help them out as much as possible. So if we have gallery openings or exhibition openings, we will sell their work, and that money goes straight from the buyer to the artist and does not come through the organization. We take nothing off the top. If I can negotiate something with the buyer or, when we're working with CAMH, if I can negotiate an administration fee, that's a bonus. We never take 10% off the artist or anything like that. Our artists are not charged; all of our programs are free of charge. Again, accessibility is really key for us, but in regards to the employment opportunities, it's about giving them independence.

We've been working really closely with ODSP (Ontario Disability Support Program) to make sure our artists don't get penalized for the money they make trying to start their career. They've been incredible at helping our artists set up separate business accounts that they can put their expenses into or get their expenses out of and put their earnings directly into these business accounts, so they don't get penalized as an individual with a personal account.

We also have an incredible relationship with Equity, which is the Theatre Union of Canada. We have an equally incredible relationship with Actra—they work with film and television actors. We connect our artists with them to help our people get started with their career. Membership dues, fees, taxes: all these things can be really expensive and may deter somebody from trying out this line of work. Through simple outreach and conversations with these organizations, we've been able to strike up some really great partnerships and again continue a really great conversation about artists trying to break into this field.

Angela: That's amazing. Now, I know that you've got other programs as well; we've covered a little bit of the film festival; and now we've covered a little bit of musicians and their music. But one of the stats that I had mentioned was that writers are 121% more likely to suffer from bipolar disorder. What kind of programs do you have for writers specifically?

Danica: We've been working with Bill Bisset, who is a sound poet in Canada. He's been around since the 1960s. He is incredible; such a cool human being. We've had an incredible poetry program with Workman Arts. He was our poet in residence for about four or five years, and we put out a poetry anthology where our artists were paid to get published and received copies of their book. That book is available for sale through our website as well. It was published by

CAMH, which is another fantastic resource that they've provided us with.

We also work with Robert Huff, who is an incredible Toronto novelist. Again, it's about holding people to a standard that is realistic. We don't want our artists to be creating in a bubble so that when they leave to try to get work outside of Workman Arts there's a barrier that we've created just by trying to support them in our isolated community. We want to provide high-end academic training courses that will pull them up to a level that will actually benefit them in the long run. Robert Huff has created some excellent workshops—actual real workshops—where they can critique and help develop each other's work.

Many literary artists have also started out in a program that I started a couple of years ago called *Theatre Ensemble*. Theatre is my background; it's my baby. This is the reason that I love Workman Arts: it's because I can start these kinds of programs.

It started off as a literary course of play writing, writing for the stage. So we took our literary artists—again the best of literary artists—and put them through a series of training programs that would help them create for the stage. Not just script writing, but more abstract thinking about what it is to create for the stage. We then brought in actors.

We started the workshop on top of that work, the original work written by our artists. We then had our actors and our literary artists working together in creating original pieces. Then we brought in some visual artists and media artists to help with the design aspect. We brought in an incredible designer, Glenn

Davidson; we've been working with Kate Lashington, an incredible playwright in Toronto. Actually, her daughter, Natasha Greenblad, is a great actress and director. It's absolutely incredible to have a mother-daughter duo working on such a great project. We've also been working with Kit Tough, another incredible Toronto artist.

One thing we pride ourselves on is hiring currently active, working artists in the Toronto arts community. It helps us create a bridge for our artists to get into the community because if an instructor comes, and they bond and collaborate with one of our artists, they might use them in future projects. They might come to them for more work opportunities. Again, we don't want to get instructors who, if you can't do, teach: that's not going to serve anybody or anyone. We want people who are currently active, who are in on the newer trends, not just old traditions. So a lot of what I like to do is to get different disciplines working with other disciplines.

Another thing we did was to take literary artists and partner them with visual artists to create illustrated stories. We bring people out of their comfort zone. You don't grow unless you're taken out of your comfort zones. To get other artists working with each other, thinking out different ways that they can support each other and collaborate—that's what I love to do. That's the challenge that I really enjoy.

We're currently working on a digital storytelling program that will bring photographers into a more media arts-related discipline and focus. Digital storytelling is huge right now. It's also quite accessible. You don't need a lot of equipment; you don't need a lot of technical knowledge to be able to edit these things and put them together. Again, accessibility, collaboration and—for me—bringing the different disciplines together, is a really big part of the programming work that I do.

Angela: OK. Now, just another aspect of things here. I'm wondering…you must have a program for dancers. Because you're a dancer, right?

Not only does she sing, but yes, she dances too!

Danica: We've done a lot of different programs: movement for theatre or movement for actors. Having a connection with your body is huge in mental health and addiction recovery. Just to be a healthy person in general, to have a healthy relationship with your body, your movement is a key element. We've partnered a lot with Moynan King. He's an incredible movement instructor in Toronto.

Creating a trust with your body, a trust in physical space and in those around you, in order to create different things is a huge aspect. There were some incredible things that came out of that.

One of our original productions, *Third Eye Looming*—which is how I got involved with the organization to begin with—is a production that was created through a collaboration of artists who share their stories. And, not too surprising, as soon as you start sharing stories, you start realizing common ground, common visions that people have through different parts of their psychosis or through their mania. Common experiences with the law; with mental health organizations; with incarceration; with family members; what happens to your family when you are mentally ill; what happens to the relationships with your family when you get become ill.

A group of artists got together and they shared their stories and we worked with Ed Roy. I love Ed Roy. He is fantastic. I cannot stress this enough: he's an incredible creator, he's an incredible human being, and he facilitated this whole discussion and created a sixteen minute movement piece called *Third Eye Looming*. The whole piece is set to a video projection that helps to illustrate psychosis, which can be very difficult to describe. It also was developed as an easy way to tour the production. There's not a stick of furniture, there's no set, there's no scenery, and there are minimal costumes and make up.

The first time we did it we had a cast of seven, and the last time we did it we had a cast of six. It's about getting up for a day of work, and just having your world crumble around you. Going through paranoia, delusions, and incarceration. We had this piece originally go to Amsterdam as part of the third Madness and Arts World Festival. This festival was started by Workman Arts in 2003. In 2006, it went to Munster, Germany and in 2010 it was in Harlem, Netherlands.

We took this piece to Harlem, Netherlands and then remounted it back in April 2014 as part of the *Abilities Arts Festival* at the Daniel Spectrum Theatre. We remounted it as full Equity production which, again, is another great paid opportunity for our artists—great contract work—when you work with Equity. Everything is unionized and you get to work with the best of the best. And that was another dance piece. So, again, we had to get everyone fit. We had hardcore workouts every day for six days a week. That's six hours a day that you are dancing, moving and collaborating.

And even though Ed Roy is the director, he's a creator and director, so he's open to everyone's additions and ideas. That's hard for a director. You don't get that in a director very often. He plays to everyone's strengths, and he understands people's weaknesses. And, again, that is something that you do not get in professional theatre very often at all: if you can't do it, you're asked to leave and they will find a replacement. That just doesn't exist in this environment that we've created, which is astounding and we've gotten from him, too, that it's great experience to be in on the other side of the table as well. It's fantastic and beautiful how these kinds of opportunities attract the best of the best that are out there. Again, we had the best designer, with the best lighting guy, with the best stage manager, etc. Things that you wouldn't normally think of. It really just attracted the best people out there.

For movement, dance is not specifically part of our mandate. However, something super cool coming up: we'll be partnering with a dance company in Montreal on a project called *Un Coup Pour Voir* which will be put up during the 2014 Summer Works Festival, the Theatre Festival in Toronto in August, and it's one of our productions. It's a one-on-one presentation. So a dancer will walk up to you, hand you a set of headphones, and give you a two-and-a-half minute presentation. We're targeting places where festival-goers will be in line at a beer tent, or in a park near of the theatres that will be hosting the festival. And you'd go with a single iPod with really long extended cables for the headset, and you have an experience. In the way that I've heard it described, it's not a performance: it's a shared experience, it's a gift, it's an offering. The reason they wanted to work with us was because there are a thousand dance companies in Toronto, but they're tired of working with dancers, because they know what they're going to get. They want to work with storytellers, people who are interested in speaking about their experiences or showing their experiences in different ways. I'm actually holding all of the auditions tomorrow in our space. I'll be filming them all to send over to Montreal and cast three or four dancers or movers who are interested in telling a story with their bodies. So as opposed to ballet or modern or tap, we're looking at movement as a form of abstract expression.

Angela: That's fantastic. That is so cool. I'm going to leave it there because that was awesome! Danica is such a wonderful, amazing, very warm, interesting, and very well-spoken human being. I am so appreciative that you are here tonight. Before we sign off, please give me your websites again and let me know how people can contact the organization.

Danica: So I am Danica Brown and I can be reached through our website:

http://www.workmanarts.com

You'll find out all the information on the different training programs that we provide; you can see biographies on our instructors, different collaborators and partners, as well as all my contact information. You can contact us any time. Shoot me an email or send me a phone call. Unfortunately, right now we do have a bit of a waiting list, but I never like to leave somebody with a flat "no." There are other like-minded organizations. Unfortunately, a lot of funding has fallen apart, but there's still a lot out there. A lot of community centres will offer things.

We are best suited for artists interested in performing professionally, developing their arts practice as opposed to just picking up a paintbrush for the first time and wanting to test things out. But if that's where you're at, we have lots of connections for those kinds of programs as well. So again, contact me through our website, my phone number and my email address are accessible through there within the contact information.

Getting Lost In The System Part I

In this chapter, Angela interviews Julie, the mother of a young girl who has struggled with mental illness difficulties since the age of two. They discuss their battles and frustration with the healthcare system, getting her daughter diagnosed properly and receiving the proper treatment she needs. This episode highlights the most common problems of having a child with a mental illness and a society that hasn't been educated about mental illness.

Julie lives a busy life working while managing her challenging child. She is able to work and exercise from home in order to be available to her family. Her daughter requires constant interaction and parental support, which is why Julie's voice is important for parents to hear.

This interview was first recorded August, 2013.

Angela: Welcome to *Different from the Other Kids*, relevant for anybody who has a child with mood difficulties. I'm here tonight talking to Julie.

I found this really interesting piece in the Toronto Star—Interesting because it reminded me of Julie's story. What was really interesting to me was the plight of parents trying to get help with their daughter who experiences different shifts and different episodes of mentally ill-type behaviour. Julie and her husband Ian have been trying to get help for their daughter who has a mental illness. I found this article in the Toronto Star, and it's excellent because it totally captured what is happening to so many parents, at least in the province of Ontario, Canada.

According to the Toronto Star, in an article by Laura Armstrong, Sunline Airlines had to turn around a plane about forty-five minutes into a flight on Friday morning after a passenger allegedly made a direct threat to the aircraft. They had two fighter jets from NORAD, which they dispatched to escort the flight carrying one hundred and eighty-three passengers and a crew of six back to Pearson Airport. This young man, who is twenty-five years old, suffered from depression for years and needs help for both mental and physical health issues. According to the father, he and his wife have called the police on their son twenty-three times after verbal altercations, hoping to get him some treatment. Unfortunately they didn't help. Every time, "I told them he has illness. He has mental problems. Nobody helped." His Dad is now relieved. "This is unbelievable to me. This is actually a relief, because now my son will be assessed by a hospital and (placed) under a seventy-two hour hold."

My frustration is—and Julie will hear me when I say—I can't believe it actually took the incarceration of this young man for him to get the help he needs. Julie and I have had conversations about sending her daughter in the right direction to try and get some resources. She hits brick walls constantly. She goes somewhere, all she gets is a "no" and a door shut, and her child is still undiagnosed. She's now medicated, but that's very recent.

I've never heard of anybody going through what Julie and Ian have been through. I'm very happy that they're here. I'm very sad for their story. If you don't mind, Julie, I'd love to ask you to just give us a general synopsis of how you knew at one point or another that you were having difficulty with your child.

Julie: I think it was somewhere around the age of two. We saw signs that something was not quite right, but we didn't act on anything because you kind of go into denial as a parent, and you think, "Oh, it's just a phase. It'll pass." But I think around the age of two, I saw the first sign, and I'll never forget it. I was doing Sophie's hair and I came around the front of her. I knelt down in front of her and I looked her in the eye and I said, "Oh, you look so beautiful." I remember she scowled at me, she put her hands in her hair and she messed it up and stomped out the room.

It was my first indication that there was something not quite right. From there, we always noticed that she wasn't able to have or maintain friendships. She struggled in school, and we weren't really sure of all the struggles because we had her in a Montessori program up until the age of eight. We thought that she was thriving in that program, and then we put her in the public school program. We then realized that she was not thriving; she was way below grade level, at which time we started looking for assessments. We put her in tutoring programs through Oxford (a private tutoring school), trying to bring her up to grade level, but she just wasn't able to catch up.

Angela: When someone has a mental illness or mood disorder, it is very common to have a learning disability. Did they tell you she had a learning disability?

Julie: No.

Angela: So nobody gave you a diagnosis or anything?

Julie: No.

Julie: Finally, in 2011, we sought out a neuropsychologist to have a neuropsych evaluation done. We learned that she had very slow processing disorder; she was in the fourth percentile. Very slow working memory. And they said she was suffering from anxiety and depression. She was extremely rigid in her thought structure. She would stay stuck on the same course, even after her strategy was failing. She would continue the same thought. She wasn't able to look outside of that and try something new.

Angela: At what point would you say things escalated? When she became a teenager, I'm guessing?

Julie: Yes, she was always explosive. She could be unkind to me, certainly; and to her dad. But more so to me, just because I was more available to her. I can't remember now what she used to say, but I can always remember the way she would make me feel. I can remember being in the shower in the morning and having this great anxiety about being able to get through that shower before she woke up, because if she woke up and I was unavailable to her, she would be in a rage that I wasn't there and I didn't hear her call. I just had this feeling of anxiety that I always felt if I wasn't doing what she wanted me to be doing or I wasn't available to her.

Angela: At what point did it escalate that you knew you had your hands full to the point where you needed more help than just tutors?

Julie: Well, it's a process. I remember going to her GP and being in her office crying, saying, "Something's wrong. I don't know what it is." She sent me to a pediatrician. I think she was around nine at that point, and the pediatrician put her on Prozac, which didn't help at all. Throughout it all she kept escalating and her social life was just deteriorating. She was having drama everywhere. She just cannot connect with people; she cannot function socially. The more drama she encounters outside of the home, the more drama she brings into the home, and it's just… it just keeps going to the point where she's putting holes in the walls and screaming. She's threatening the dog; she's threatening herself. It's just complete chaos.

Angela: And when she's threatening, if you don't mind, specifically, what is threatening?

Julie: Well, it got bad enough to occur to her that grabbing a knife out of the drawer and sort of, you know, slyly looking at it and saying, "This one will do." She was holding it up to me like she was going to stab me with it. She held an ice skate over her head and threatened her dad she was going to cut herself with it.

Angela: So, give me a synopsis of the last year. You and I have only been in contact for the last year, and it has been unbelievable to me what you've had to do, where it is that you've gone, to the extent that you have gone and still gotten nothing. So I want to make sure that we hit the right point here, and that is that you've gone to a bunch of different places that I thought would have been able to help you at some point, and you haven't really received any concrete help. Go through some of the places that you've been to. I've sent you to a couple of places to try, but still nothing helps.

Julie: We finally got access to a psychiatrist in early 2010. She prescribed Abilify and Prozac, which did stabilize her for a period of time. We had about nine month's stability. And then it seemed that at some point that medication stopped working, and she escalated to a great deal of violence. She was just falling apart everywhere.

Angela: When you say violence, what would that entail?

Julie: Throwing, hitting, punching. There was a lot of self-loathing.

Angela: That's terrible.

Julie: She would threaten to kill herself; say that she didn't want to live and that she was going to cut herself.

Angela: It can be lonely as parents, difficult and terrible, and I appreciate you sharing your story. It's very brave and really is appreciated. I do believe there are people sitting by themselves, not able to have a conversation with anyone. Thank you for sharing that much.

Julie: No problem. So after about nine months on the cocktail of medications, she was on Adderall, because at some point during all of this she was diagnosed with ADHD and we put her in a private school. The teacher would be in touch and say she wouldn't be on task, she'd lose focus, she was not able to accomplish anything. So we had her on Abilify, Prozac and Adderall, which felt like quite a cocktail to us.

After nine months she was on this medication, things started to get out of hand again to the point where one night we had to call the police because she was threatening us. So we left the home. After we left the home, she was calling us on our cell phones to say she was going to kill herself. As parents we had to plug back in; we had to come home. She was only thirteen and threatening us and herself. She was just a very unstable person. So we went back to the psychiatrist who was prescribing the medicine, and we said, "This is not working because we had to call the police. This is what's happening in our home." We said that perhaps we should take her off all of this medication and she agreed.

After that it just got worse. She became intolerable, unbearable; and it was two to three months of this nightmare, the craziest time we had ever endured. During that time we were calling COAST (Crisis Outreach and Support Team) a lot, which is the local crisis line.

Angela: COAST is a police officer in plain clothes and a social worker that work as an outreach team in our area. They come into the house, and if the person in question requires hospitalization then the social worker is able to do an intake, and if they require incarceration for whatever reason, whatever's going on in the home, then the police officer is there. I've met them through two different incidents. One of them was just a house call when my daughter got back from the hospital, and the other was for an unbalanced mother of a friend. In my experience they were excellent. Were they really great with you, too?

Julie: Well, they took three or four phone calls before I could actually get them to our home, because they would talk to you, then they would say, "Well, let us talk to Sophie." So they would de-escalate the situation, and they would tell us they didn't have a team available. It took three or four calls to Coast before I finally had a team come to our home. They were fantastic, and it was finally through that contact that we got in contact with a nurse practitioner who worked for COAST and for another service in our city. They finally called me one day on a follow-up, and we had a ten minute conversion on the phone. She said, "This is the medication she needs to be on." She dropped off the prescription the next day.

Angela: That's unbelievable. I've never heard of such a thing.

Julie: I know.

Angela: I mean, thank God something finally gave, but still, to have someone from our healthcare system prescribe something and drive it to your home, that's pretty great.

Julie: She prescribed Zoloft and Seroquel; it has changed things dramatically. Things are not perfect, but it's certainly calmed things down and de-escalated the violent and suicidal sort of chatter.

Angela: So she has been more balanced and stable, mood-wise, since she started taking the medication?

Julie: Yes, the last three weeks.

Angela: I know Sophie has some attachment issues with her parents, but she's gone to a camp called Camp Kodiak recently; it's in Ontario. Tell us about that experience a little bit, about Camp Kodiak.

Julie: It's called Camp Kodiak, and it's a specialized camp that caters to kids between the ages of eight and eighteen with or without a diagnosis or learning disability, but it also takes mainstream kids. It is focused on social skills and teamwork. The minimum length of stay for any child is three weeks, and we dropped her off yesterday to stay.

Angela: You've been so stressed in the past six months. So how are you feeling? Sophie gone to camp for three weeks must be great.

Julie: Well, I'm a mess. I'm full of anxiety because I don't know what's happening, and I'm concerned about whether or not she's fitting in, if she's liking it, and if she's feeling safe and secure. So I'm crazy when she's here, and I'm crazy when she's not. That's really what it comes down to.

Angela: Do you have an idea of how many hospital visits you've been to?

Julie: Her last hospital visit was July 1st. Sophie woke up that morning, and we were not even out of our bed. She came into our room threatening us; she was threatening herself; she was threatening the dog. We had been through this daily, for a couple of weeks, with many daily calls to COAST and to the police. So we said, "That's it. We're going to the hospital." So we got ready. We went.

Angela: Did Sophie agree to go to the hospital visit to receive help?

Julie: Yes, she wanted to go. She felt out of control and very unstable, so she very willingly went. We got through four layers of staff. We got through triage, the emergency doctor and then a mental health team which was a man and a woman, then, finally, the child psychiatrist. And when we got to the child psychiatrist, she told us that we clearly did not meet criteria for an admission. I think a lot of it is because when Sophie presents, she is so calm and composed, and she's able to say, "I feel sad, I feel unhappy." It's just…it's nuts. So, anyway, the child psychiatrist told us we did not meet the criteria for admission and told us that we were going to be sent home, and that if things escalated again we needed to use emergency services.

Angela: There's got to be something different that we can do in these cases, because the unfortunate side to all this is that in order for most people to achieve a diagnosis they have to risk their life or the life of someone around them in order to receive the proper help. It's just unacceptable. Apparently you have to have NORAD come after you, and you have to have a plane with one hundred and eighty-three people that gets turned around, and a SWAT team that come onto the plane before you get any kind of mental help. The parents went to the hospital twenty-three times, I don't know how many times you went in the last six months, but you reached out for help a lot. I just don't know how to swallow it anymore. As a society it's unacceptable. Many people recommend that you write a journal. Is that something you do, in order to have a timeline?

Julie: After our visit to the GP, she said to me, "You need a story. You need to have a story so that if you have to go to the hospital again, if you have to call 911, you have a piece of paper which has dates and diagnoses and interventions and everything written down." So I do have a story. It's about two pages long, and if I ever need it, I actually have it in the glove box of my car.

Angela: I just wanted to ask from another parent's perspective, because I feel like sometimes I'm so busy trying to keep up with what's going on. I just don't know at times if I'm doing the right thing. It's good to know someone else's experiences like yours with Sophie, because I would have never believed, if you didn't tell me, that documenting the episodes would help.

I wanted to say before we end this episode, be careful in Canada. They see a child psychiatrist, then they go into the adult system. My daughter was very stable at eighteen and so, in between those ages of going into the adult system, we kept talking about getting another doctor, an adult psychiatrist. And I kept saying, "Yeah, we have to do that." We had our name on a list at one point, but she had an episode within six months of turning nineteen, which is the cap-off age for them to see a child psychiatrist. I was very lucky that they had started this outpatient psychiatric unit at my local hospital, otherwise I'm not really sure what would've happened. Make sure that you have everything looked after before eighteen, then you know you're not going to be left without a source of help.

Julie: I also wanted to tell everyone about this online support group. It's called

http://www.conductdisorders.com

It's a place where you can post and receive support and advice, and I have found it to be very helpful. Sometimes it gives me great hope when you read success stories, and sometimes it gives me great fear because there are a lot of people who don't have a happy story to tell. But it's always good to know that you're not alone and to receive some support and advice. It's people from all over the world supporting you and your struggles. There are people from Morocco and across the United States that are posting there.

Angela: We're going to sign off for now. Julie, I thank you. I really appreciate your honesty. I appreciate your courage to be able to come out here and tell your story. I know there are people on the other end, like me, who really appreciate that.

Additional Resources

Angela and her guests have put together a collection of resources to help parents of challenging children. It includes nutrition and exercise advice, checklists and other useful tips and information.

You can get a copy by visiting

http://www.dftok.com/bonus-page

Getting Lost In The System Part II

In this chapter Angela interviews Ian, the husband of Julie and father of Sophie from chapter nine. Julie talked a lot about Sophie's struggles and history. She touched on the topic of getting lost in the system. Ian is here to tell us about both the father's and husband's perspective; the lack of support in our health-care system; and how it actually takes someone threatening a life to get the help they need.

Ian is a VP of Sales and Marketing for a firm near Toronto, Ontario. We wanted to hear from Ian, the sole male parent in this effort so far, on how he deals with the challenges of managing a high-pressure professional life, with an equally (if not more) high-pressure home life.

This interview was first recorded August, 2013.

Angela: Welcome Ian. For those who don't know, Ian's daughter, although not diagnosed, struggles with some mental illness issues. She has mental illness episodes. Julie and Ian have reached out many times to a lot of different segments of the mental health community, looking for help and, unfortunately, have received very little.

This is a story I have heard told over and over again. In the last interview, we spoke of a story in the paper of a young man who had been on a plane from Toronto, just about a week ago, and it took

NORAD, two fighter jets and a SWAT team to bring in a plane with one hundred and eighty-three people so that this young man could be taken into custody. Believe it or not, the young man's father was thrilled. I can't even imagine being thrilled that my son was being incarcerated. That was a real story of a real family that was helped only when the young person threatened to bring down a passenger plane.

Can you give me a short background of when you knew your daughter was having some challenges?

Ian: When Sophie was two, Julie was working from home and had seen something a little bit odd in Sophie. One day Julie was doing Sophie's hair. Julie said Sophie looked beautiful, so she said, "Wow! You just look terrific!" Sophie looked at her, had a little scowl on her face and messed up her hair completely and shot her a dirty look. That was one of the first signs that we felt that something was definitely 'off' with her. She definitely didn't have a regular response to a compliment, and it progressed from there. Now we have been to doctors, we've been to a psychiatrist and psychologist, she's had brain scans, all to try and pinpoint what the challenge might be. It has been very frustrating, to be honest. The biggest challenge I'm finding is with the system. Getting the help that you need for your child can be impossible.

A good example is the young man on the flight to Panama. As Angie referenced earlier, his parents went twenty-three times to the hospital and finally this guy gets help because he threatens to take down a plane. The system is fractured, and that's been the most frustrating part for me. We've been to the hospital, to the ER, twice. Both times they didn't admit her. It's partially understandable, because Sophie manages to bring her behaviour down to a certain level and presents herself very well in front of a professional. To a certain extent, I can see why they would send us home, but they're not living in the home. They're not seeing what we're going through. They don't see the knife come out of the drawer and the threat to kill us and then kill herself. I don't think there's nearly enough resources spent on this kind of thing. You read the stats: one in five kids now suffers from some sort of mental illness. We're experiencing that first-hand, and it's not fun. I would love to get to a two-tiered healthcare system.

Angela: Ian is an entrepreneur, and I'd love to hear what you would like to see from a two-tiered health system in Canada.

Ian: Just the option for people to have the ability to go to a private psychiatrist. We should have that option. Ultimately that helps everybody in the system, because if I can pay for a service, it frees up the queue below me for other people that can't afford to pay to use the 'free' health care. It benefits everybody in the entire system. Why we continue to roadblock these things is beyond me. It's not an "I'm-better-than-you" system, it's just that I have the ability to help free-up the system. I will pay for that and I'm fine with that.

Angela: You went into the emergency room not long ago and begged for the hospital to hold Sophie. She was in such a bad mental space that she was willing to stay in, that particular time. The hospital said, "I am sorry she doesn't hit the criteria, you have to take her home." You want some help for parents that seek it for children with mental illness.

Ian: It was ridiculous because, as you said, Sophie was willing to stay. Julie was very emotional because we felt we had finally reached a threshold where we needed to reach out. We thought we were going to get the help that we needed.

Angela: They sent you home with no support. How many days was she really unstable?

Ian: I would say she was really unstable for about six months. It was daily, and it was constant.

Angela: What did the day look like?

Ian: I hated coming home; I would rather be at work. I hated the weekends because I knew it was going to be hard. Sophie didn't have any friends; we were going to be the entertainment, and it was just awful. Stuff was getting thrown everywhere. The vacuum's getting thrown downstairs, things are getting thrown in your face, knives are being pulled out of drawers. There wasn't a point at which we could relax. It just wasn't a good time for Julie and me. We decided at that time we were going to send Sophie to camp this summer. We desperately needed a break from her. We found a camp that included children and youth with Learning Disabilities, ADHD, NCD and high functioning Asperger's. They were willing to take Sophie for three weeks.

Angela: Camp Kodiak is the name of the camp, and it is being attended by quite a few children from all over the United States. There's one from Israel, one from Norway. I know it is a good camp. It's a big financial responsibility, isn't it?

Ian: Well, this three week program costs five thousand dollars. We started off by checking-in at the medical building because you want to check and make sure that everybody has their meds. We met a woman in front of us who was from Washington D.C., and she had done a lot of research; all the reviews were great. But yes, it's expensive. This is the kind of thing that should be available for everybody, not just people that can afford to pay.

Angela: Did you guys ever run across anything that you could do for respite care for a weekend? For an evening?

Ian: We really relied on family for the most part for our support, and lucky for us we have a great family. They've been very supportive. But Sophie has burned a lot of those bridges now. Some of the sources that we had, being family members, are now no longer available to us.

Angela: In Ontario, there are certain hospitals that specialize in certain things, but if you are not in the right geographical area, then they cannot help you.

Ian: The program in Hamilton is Contact Hamilton. We've been on the waiting list. We had interviews with people, and even after we told them everything we are still looking at many months wait to get in for help.

Angela: Eight months.

Ian: We were in crisis mode at the time we approached them. It was crazy that they told us we had to wait another eight months. It's just ridiculous to us. Further to your point, if there are other services available at Sunnybrook (a hospital about fifty minutes away) why can't we go there? We're all paying into the healthcare system for Ontario, but we're not in that catchment; we fall under Hamilton, and that's where we have to go. So we patiently waited. We've done our thing here, and we are still in line, about a month or two away. We did finally get through to somebody (while on the waiting list), and then we had the nurse practitioner come to our home and prescribe new medication.

It was interesting. It seemed out of the blue. This nurse came to us and said she had been reviewing our file. She just showed up at the house, and that was the start of getting some help. We are finally making some progress through Contact Hamilton, but it has been a painstakingly long process. Again, let's flashback to the guy in the plane: his father brought him for help at the hospital twenty-three times and left with nothing. The system is broken.

Angela: Can you take us through what an episode looks like for Sophie.

Ian: She becomes very angry, and it can be the smallest thing that sets her off. People always ask what sets her off, but there isn't any particular trigger.

Angela: Interesting, she really doesn't have one.

Ian: She doesn't have one that would make sense to me. The most recent incident that is burned in my brain was somewhat violent. Sophie was being very belligerent and rude and mean and wanted Julie to come in and say good night to her. Julie told her, "No, I'm not going to come out and say good night to you. You've been rude and mean. Just go to bed, and we'll take it up again in the morning."

We were sitting out in the backyard. She started kicking the glass door, the sliding door, kicking it to the point that we thought it was going to break then she locked us out of the house. We got up and walked around the side of the house. She had lost sight of us, and that gave her more anxiety, so we entered through the side door. We came bursting in and grabbed the keys to the house. As Julie went out back outside, I came through the kitchen. Sophie was standing there and said, "I'm going to kill the three of you," meaning the two of us and our dog. She pulled a large bread knife out of the drawer, held it up at me, and said, "Yep, this will do." She was extremely angry. I told her, "I'm calling 911." Those are the only options we have available to us. Saying that I was going to call the police brought her back down to a less violent level.

Angela: What happens, when you go back to the psychiatrist and tell them this?

Ian: It's so hard to explain because she does put on such a brave face in front of the professionals and seems quite fine. Because of further threats to our life, Sophie agreed to come with us in the car, and we took her to the emergency room that night. I explained the whole knife story to the psychiatrist on call at the time, and it just didn't seem to go anywhere.

Angela: Were you under the care of another psychiatrist outside the hospital?

Ian: We were.

Angela: OK, what happens when you to see the psychiatrist that she sees regularly? The one she's a patient of?

Ian: That's another story altogether.

Ian: We were dealing with a Port Credit (part of the Greater Toronto Area) psychiatrist. She was referred to us through a pediatrician in Burlington, so we thought, "Great. Finally we had a breakthrough. We are now seeing a full-fledged medical illness professional."

This was a couple of years ago. The psychiatrist prescribed Abilify, Prozac and another med—Julie knows it a whole lot better than I do. They didn't seem to be helping, so we wanted to take Sophie off the medication. The doctor wasn't necessarily agreeing with us, but didn't really urge us to keep her on or take her off. If she would have said at that time not to do it I would have agreed, but we had it kind of in our minds that, "Let's strip her down and see where we are and what we're dealing with." The psychiatrist didn't say, "No, that's a terrible idea." She walked us through how should we wean her off—which was far too quickly, according to research that we've done since! We took her off the Abilify too fast, which was not a good thing at all. We got her back on the meds pretty quickly after, and we reached out to the psychiatrist in Port Credit. When we went to see her, she threw her hands up and said, "I'm done with you guys, I suggest you work with someone else."

Angela: How long were you with her?

Ian: Two years.

Angela: I don't get how a psychiatrist could throw in the towel, so to speak.

Ian: She had the ability to prescribe meds beneficial to Sophie, but when it came to the therapy she was terrible.

Angela: Did you ever use a psychologist?

Ian: We did have a psychologist. A fantastic psychologist. She is the best, and she seems to get through to Sophie and help but it's… again, once we walk out that door everything changes. Sophie forgets everything that they talked about.

Angela: I know that you have some pretty strong opinions about what you'd like to see handled different in the mental health community. What is it that you'd like to say to them?

Ian: Like I said before, go back to some privatization. Give us the option to get help and then free up the queue below us for other people to get the resources throughout the province. That is the biggest fault of the system. My stepfather went through diagnosis and cancer treatment, and I have to say the healthcare system was fantastic. It was unbelievable. He had great care. Why don't we have that on the mental health side? In my mind, it is as big an issue as cancer is. I was with him when he went through his cancer treatments, and I was very impressed. Princess Margaret and Trillium (hospitals in the Greater Toronto Area that both specialize in cancer treatment) gave him fantastic service.

I expected the same treatment when we went through this with Sophie. I was shocked to see that it is nowhere near the same. Eight months waiting for some help, being threatened constantly, being sent away to fend for ourselves and our sick daughter. Back to the guy in the plane: his parents took him to the hospital looking for help twenty-three times. It teaches people that you only get help when you do something serious. What's it going to take? It shouldn't be this way.

Angela: You had mentioned earlier something about that woman at the camp from the US; she had done lots of research and even met the owner of the camp and had high hopes for a good experience. She was tired of spending money for services that weren't meeting the needs of the child.

Ian: US healthcare is similar to our system, but they have the ability to get private healthcare. In that parent's case, was it the psychiatrist? Was it the system? Was she talking to the right people?

Angela: That's unfortunate. That's what psychiatrists are supposed do.

Ian: But often, they just prescribe meds.

Angela: In Canada, they are pharmacological consultants more than they are actual shrinks.

Ian: You need to be both. We need to find that balance between both because you can teach these kids the general information about what they are suffering from. What they really need is someone to teach them coping strategies and how to deal with difficult thoughts.

Angela: Is going to the hospital or calling 911 the only thing that would help her calm down?

Ian: Yes.

Angela: Anything else work?

Ian: Authority and public humiliation. Bringing in somebody from the outside. That worked. We had an issue recently. We took her for a horseback ride and she wasn't in a good place, was very unhappy, wasn't going to get out of the car. That was not an option. We were all in a bad place, so we just rolled down the windows. It was only when a kid around her age came by who was part of the family that runs the horseback riding place, and as soon as Sophie realized I wasn't moving and she was going to have to explain why she was in the car and not participating, did she get out of the car. Sophie puts on this very stoic, brave face; doesn't want to be embarrassed publicly.

Angela: So she does display some control. I would imagine that there's a primary diagnosis and I'm guessing a comorbid diagnosis to go along with it. I'm guessing this particular diagnosis is very difficult because of her age, and because she's female. As I understand it—and I'm sorry to tell you this—it's about twenty-four when young woman's hormones and chemicals calm down enough that they become who they are going to be.

Ian: Great! Ten more years!

Angela: Yes, sorry about that. And something else I can tell you from experience: she can be stable for a while and then won't be. It is dependent on chemicals, hormones and even nutrition. Any change in her body and the meds can stop working.

Ian: Couldn't agree with that more. The Abilify seemed to be the magic drug for a period of time. As she turned thirteen, things completely went off the rails, as if the Abilify was no longer effective. As you've just said, she could have outgrown that medication and we have to try something different.

Angela: That apparently can happen at any time; someone feels very stable for thirty years with the aid of medication, and then all of a sudden something changes and they go off into an episode of some kind.

Ian: It's surprising you said that, because that happened to my aunt on my side of the family. We always blame my side of the family for Sophie's challenges because there's definitely history there.

Angela: There's usually history on both sides. One side is often more prevalent, but there is definitely a genetic component that goes along with all of these challenges.

Ian: My Aunt that we are talking about spiralled out of control after she had her first and only child. They did finally stabilize her. She was suicidal. It was terrible. She would go to the liquor store buy a bottle of vodka and just sit in the parking lot and down it. She was in a truly bad place. They medicated her, stabilized her and, as you said it can happen, for about thirty years she was fine, and then I'm guessing she got menopausal. At that stage of her life, again, she went off the rails. Now she's fine, functioning, but again medicated.

Angela: Let's talk about the jobless rate for those that are mentally ill. I can see exactly what happens with the mentally ill at different times now. With my daughter, we go through periods of time of stability, and all of a sudden there's an episode, she loses her job, she loses her boyfriend, she spends all her money, she drinks too much and she's on the couch for periods of time, not getting up. When I say "not getting up," I mean, not getting up to shower, never mind get a job. After being ill for a while, her mood starts to stabilize and she goes right back to the self-loathing thing. At that point, she has such low confidence, she doesn't do very much. It's really awful to watch. Apparently, the jobless rate in the US (at least according to USA Today) is eighty percent.

Ian: Eighty percent!

Angela: Just to add a glimmer of hope, I just spoke to a young woman who works for a program for the arts that employs people who are mentally ill and <u>only</u> people that are mentally ill. They are funded through arts programs in Ontario. They are not funded through mental health programming. Have you heard of very many programs for work for the mentally ill?

I don't have extended health benefits for myself or Christina, and presently I'm at about eleven hundred dollars for my one daughter a month. This includes meds, counselling, and teeth and eyes. I'm not sure how long we're going to be able to do this, but she has to have the medication, which is the biggest part of the expense. Hopefully I will get her out on her own, and then she can apply for some kind of a government subsidy. This is unmanageable if she were on her own with no help.

I just want to say thanks so much to Ian. I really appreciate you coming to speak to me. I think it's brave for parents to come forward and share their stories. There are a lot of people out there with absolutely no support, a lot of people with nobody to talk to, and a lot of parents out there that probably don't have the resources to get help. This effort is for them. You are not alone.

Ian: Thank you for having me Angie, I think what you're doing here is a fantastic thing to get the message out to people. They're not alone and there's a light at the end of the tunnel.

Additional Resources

Angela and her guests have put together a collection of resources to help parents of challenging children. It includes nutrition and exercise advice, checklists and other useful tips and information.

You can get a copy by visiting

http://www.dftok.com/bonus-page

It Takes Two

In this chapter, we speak to Julie and Ian, a loving couple who work together to care for their daughter, who has a mood disorder. They offer some great insight into how to lead a healthy lifestyle and how to balance the needs of their daughter with the demands of everyday life.

Julie and Ian have been married for over sixteen years. Many marriages are strained for couples dealing with challenging children like their daughter. We wanted to talk to them because they are defying the odds and not just staying together as a couple, but are co-parenting and keeping their relationship strong.

This interview was first recorded August, 2013.

Angela: I am very happy to be joined here by Ian and Julie, I wanted to have a conversation about what it's like to be a couple under the kind of pressure that they're under with their daughter struggling with mental and emotional challenges.

This couple is the kind of couple that you look at and are always amazed at how loving they are. They will sit and hold hands off to the side, and they communicate to one another beautifully. That's just my experience. They're laughing right now beside me, and they are always quite cute all the time. I don't know how they do it. I have never seen two parents, who are under this kind of stress with their child, be so caring and still in love. I want to find out their secrets to success. I just wanted to give everyone listening an idea of the kinds of challenges that you face as a couple under the kind of constant, daily, hourly, challenges of dealing with a child who has a disorder that is very taxing and often disruptive to your daily lives.

Welcome you guys. What do you do together in order to stay connected during your week? What are you are dealing with day in and day out?

Julie: We dine out a lot, especially as Sophie is getting older; we are able to go out and just be together. We do lunches, we do dinners, that's kind of our escape. At the beginning we knew that no matter how hard things got, divorce and separation were never an option for us. This is a serious matter, and it's not fair for only one person to go through it by themselves. This is our child, and we will stay together and do everything we can to make it right.

I think that the challenges that we face have become the glue. Some people might separate and go their different ways under these circumstances, but we've leant on each other instead. We think of this as our challenge, and it's something that we must do together. I've often thought, "I wonder, if she was 'normal', would we have as strong a marriage as we do?" I do think of it as the glue, sometimes.

Angela: OK, talk to me about vacations. Do you vacation as a family? What's that like?

Ian: We tried that one time actually. We vacationed as a family, and we all went to Bahamas with Sophie, and it just didn't go very well.

Angela: In what regard?

Julie: It was a nightmare.

Ian: She was not happy.

Angela: Is she worse out of her environment?

Ian: No, I think it was just taking that same person to a different location and the same result. Not happy; nothing was ever good enough. So for vacations now, we just vacation on our own. Again, we've been very lucky to have very supportive family. So at least once a year we give a week to ourselves. We go south or go somewhere in the US and do something on our own to recharge our batteries.

Angela: Do you both ever take separate vacation from one another? I know that you are both very close to your families.

Julie: I'll do dinners and go out with friends or with family. Ian does some weekends away with the guys to do golf where he recharges a little bit, and I've done some family spa weekends with the girls. I always feel more recharged if we do something together. I love that feeling of reconnecting and doing something just on our own. I think we come back better parents after that kind of rest.

Angela: Ian and I were talking about the ability to have good quality respite care. Julie, I never asked you this: what do you guys do when you need to get out even for just a few hours?

Ian: We're very good at keeping a balance. Like, if one of us is stressed out the other one will provide the needed support.

Julie: It's happened many times, and we're lucky that Sophie is now thirteen and we can finally walk out the door without her getting upset. What we've had to do to ensure she was safe, so we could go out, is install cameras at home. We use surveillance cameras because we used to leave the house, and she would call and threaten suicide. The cameras are our way to ensure that she won't harm herself, and allow us to leave the house and know that she is fine. We can view her via the surveillance camera on our phones.

Angela: There's probably parents out there that would love to know exactly where you set them up and what system that you used, and was it worth the cost to you?

Ian: We utilize a system called Dropcam, so if Dropcam is listening to this and want to give us some royalties that'd be great! Julie set them up. She did everything, from hooking them up to the computer to setting them up in a perfect place in the house so no one would ever know they were there.

Angela: So did they install them?

Ian: No, Julie did it all.

Julie: I did.

Ian: We just picked them up from Best Buy. It cost us around two hundred bucks for one camera and it connects to the Wi-Fi. They store the information in the cloud, it's a great system.

Angela: That's awesome.

Julie: You can move it, too. I would have it in the dining room one day and then I could move it up in the family room, depending on where she was, what she was up to before we left. We can move it. It's easy.

Angela: That's cool. That's kind of a little nannycam, if you will.

Julie: Yes.

Angela: Do you think it's a real threat when she says it?

Ian: I don't think there's really been a point that we felt that she was really going to harm herself. There have been threats and she has said that, but no, she's never tried anything. I don't think that we would really have to be concerned that she would do anything.

Julie: I always felt that it was a card she played in order to draw us back into her drama, and the camera actually was very good at letting us know that she wasn't in any danger. You could see her moving around, or listening to music, or whatever she was doing. So, she would be on the phone saying, "I'm going to hurt myself," but she would hang up the phone and then she would go and listen to The Vines on the computer. She was totally fine. So, it always felt like a card she would just play to try and draw you back.

Ian: So for those parents that are going to try and utilize the Dropcam, there is an option on the phone that lets you speak through it. We were at a restaurant at a lunch one time and accidentally clicked that button and all the restaurant noise came through, and then we saw Sophie race out the door. So, be careful when utilizing the tools available to you on that particular app.

Angela: I know that you two have the ability to somewhat work together. Julie, when you're having a hard time, how much communication are you having with Ian? How much does he want?

Julie: It is really hard, because I feel like I need his support sometimes, but at the same time I know he's the breadwinner in the family. He needs to do his job, and if I am sending him a text message saying, "Oh my God, this is crazy," then I'm taking him away from what he needs to do. I feel very torn because I do. He's my guy; like, he's the only one that I rely on constantly. I feel like I wear other people out, and he's in it with me, so it is hard not always having him there with me. I try very hard not to lean on him as much when he is working, but sometimes I need to. And of course, I feel guilty, but it's what I need at that time.

Angela: Ian, you were saying it's probably been since March that the worst stuff has been happening. How difficult is this for you to deal with work-wise?

Ian: It's been very tough. We're in a better place in the last three weeks than we have been for a long time. It was definitely affecting my job, my work; I was constantly dragged away. We're going to appointments with the psychologist and dealing with Sophie not being well, so it was definitely impactful. It's not fair for Julie to bear the burden of all that; it's not right. So you have to do what you have to do.

Angela: Now, you guys also work together to a certain extent. I don't know to what extent. So, Julie, are you able to jump in and out of your work environment? Have you been able to work at all in the last little while, and how much of a burden is that on Ian and whoever else is working with you, to make up for the fact that you are not there?

Julie: I'm extremely lucky. I have a very flexible work situation that allows me to work part-time. I have a home office, and I'm only expected in the actual office once a week. I'm only working twenty to twenty-five hours a week, and we work for the same company, but we don't have a lot of interactions. So, for me I can function and I can do what's expected of me, even though I'm very distracted by looking after Sophie.

Angela: So is that difficult for you, Ian? That must be hard to even watch. She's only in once a week, but you must sit there, pins and needles, wondering how she's going to be when she gets in, and whether she's going to be a nervous wreck after what may have happened that morning getting Sophie out the door.

Ian: Yeah, absolutely. I'll send a text message every morning saying, "How did you make out this morning, what happened?" Most of the time it's same old, "it's not been a good day." I say again, it's not fair for one person to have to bear the brunt of all that. Sophie has a lot of hostility. At this moment, it seems to be a little better, and we'll see where we go from there.

Angela: OK, so usually the kids' bedtime is a great time for couples to connect. That's usually at the end of the day, when you can sit down and have a glass of wine, or tea, or whatever and reconnect. How does that go in your house, especially with Sophie being the age that she is? She's probably not very anxious to give you that time these days. Are you able to get time at the end of the day together as a couple?

Julie: We love Seroquel.

Angela: Good answer.

Julie: Sorry.

Angela: That's funny.

Julie: Before Seroquel it was a nightmare; total nightmare. When it was time for Sophie to go to bed, the moment she would have to "completely detach," she would just escalate to this crazy, crazy place.

Angela: And how long have you been dealing with that? Has that been forever or for just the last while?

Julie: That was anytime outside of Abilify and Seroquel.

Angela: So you got two excellent sisters there with you. Ha ha!

Julie: Yes.

Angela: Some great names.

Julie: Yes, we love those anti-psychotics.

Ian: Mood stabilizers.

Julie: Mood stabilizers. It's one or the other.

Angela: So what time would she take her medication?

Julie: Now, we have her take it at around 8.30 p.m. and so at 9 o'clock she's done and she willingly goes to bed and you never hear another sound.

Angela: Well, that's awesome. So you guys actually have a life outside of her.

Ian: Well, no, because Julie also goes to bed at 9 o'clock, so I watch my MASH episode at 9.00 p.m. until 10.00 p.m. and have a glass of wine on my own.

Angela: In her defense, it's exhausting dealing with these guys all day. How about mornings? Ian, are you around in the morning or is it Julie dealing with everything?

Ian: Julie deals with Sophie in the morning because I'm usually out the door by 6.00 a.m. I like to start the day early in the office. Once or twice a week, I try to take Sophie to school to relieve Julie.

Angela: OK, cool. And Julie, how are your mornings?

Julie: Mornings are not easy. There's a great deal of hostility every morning.

Angela: She wakes up like that?

Julie: She wakes up like that almost every day.

Angela: So it start's immediately?

Julie: It starts immediately, and I will say, I'm getting really pretty good at just not letting it affect me. I walk away, but it certainly leaves a feeling of being abused and being a bit of a victim. I'm getting better. I just try not to let it stay with me all day. I have this visualization of being transparent, and whatever she's throwing at me just goes right through me.

Angela: OK, she is in school. How is that going? Does she have regular attendance at school, and does that give you some time to do the things you need to get done during the day?

Julie: Yeah.

Angela: For you, I would imagine, Ian's at work when you're not at work or you're working from home. Do you actually get some time to yourself? Does the school call you? Does she stay at home from school often? Because that's fairly common.

Julie: No, not too much. She goes to school, and she generally stays there. I do get, sometimes, a call to say she's very dark or she's negative, but for the most part she is best when she is in a structured environment. She is best when she is busy and she is with other kids, even though she might not have really successful relationships with those other kids. Any downtime is a nightmare.

Angela: Julie, twenty to twenty-five hours a week is not small. Are you able to get to the gym? What are the things that you do that keep you together, because I am really surprised. You guys have been through so much in the last little while. I know I got pretty close to a complete nervous breakdown at certain points and I'm looking at you and, no offense, but I'm thinking how much more can you take? It is all that I'm thinking. So, what do you do to combat this? What is it that you do to try and put it on an even keel?

It's a hard question that I've just asked you, I'm sorry. I can see that, but I know this will help other couples dealing with the same type of unbalance in their life. Hopefully they can take some strategies from today and implement them in their daily lives.

Julie: I know. That's OK. I do a lot. I'm a big exerciser. I walk the dog twice a day, I lift weights and I meditate.

Angela: What kind of meditation are you doing?

Julie: I do transcendental meditation.

Angela: OK, is it guided? Does that mean it's guided?

Julie: No, it's with a mantra. I took the course. I got sucked in. I think all of those things are very important and I especially love the meditation.

Angela: I'm a big meditation believer even though I'm really bad at it. How long are you meditating for and how many days a week?

Julie: My goal is everyday twice a day for twenty minutes.

Angela: Good for you.

Julie: I don't always make it. I do it at least once a day for twenty minutes.

Angela: When is best for you to do it?

Julie: You're supposed to do it in the morning and in the evening; there has to be six hours in between your meditation. When I wake up, I meditate between 6 a.m. and 6.30 a.m. and then I try and meditate again around 3 p.m., before Sophie is coming home from school or whatever activity she's in.

Angela: Regarding meditation, what did you take and where did you take it, and is it easily available? Was it online, or did you do it in person?

Julie: I Googled transcendental meditation because I heard a lot about it and I ended up finding a teacher at McMaster University, and so I went there for a four-day course.

It was very expensive and I think that I could have got where I am for a lot less money. I think that mindful meditation is just as effective as transcendental meditation. It feels—the transcendental thing—feels a little bit 'cult-y' to me, but I'm doing it and I believe in it.

Angela: Yeah, I've done a couple of meditation retreats. I went through a period of time myself where I had I guess what they would call a panic disorder, so, I was having panic attacks and I was put onto meditation. I was terrible at it. I don't think I got anywhere with the twelve week program that I did, but I went on a couple of retreats that were more helpful. They weren't overly expensive. You can find those on the internet. I do find myself even now, easily out of practice, so then I go back on to YouTube and I do guided sessions. One tool I found really good for sleep is a sound wave meditation. Have you ever done those?

Julie: No.

Angela: OK. Anyway, they're kind of cool. Ian do you meditate at all?

Julie: No.

Ian: I do not. I have Robert Mondavi as my sleep aide.

Angela: Ian's quite a guru with wine, so I'll believe that. Do you have any suggestions for somebody on the other end that wants to maintain a relationship with a challenging kid?

Ian: Suggestions? No, other than you have to really live it to understand it. We married each other because we loved each other, we have a child because we loved each other, and there's no reason that we should stop loving each other, especially now that we have a child that is needing both our help.

Julie: Highly challenging.

Ian: Highly challenging. Very great way to describe it. I don't know what to say other than, divorce is not an option. We will stick this out and figure it out as a family.

Angela: So you do family events together. You do meals together. When you are facing challenges, do you ever come up against each other with Sophie? Is there a time that your opinions split on how to deal with her?

Ian: You know, I would say that going back to the beginning, early on, I was a big proponent of spanking. I thought that this was just bad behavior, and I've been completely proven wrong. So I'm glad that we learned early that this was more than just disciplinary.

Angela: It would have been a disaster.

Ian: Exactly. I didn't go down that road.

Ian: Julie was smarter and had really researched a lot of it, and pinpointed that this was not something that's just bad behavior. It was something really different.

Angela: Well, good for both of you. It totally takes two. Julie, did you know just inherently, maternally, that that wasn't something that was going to work for this child.

Julie: It wasn't my upbringing, because I certainly was familiar with the wooden spoon! Not severely or anything, but I mean it was certainly part of my early childhood. I don't know. Sophie started to show herself as a different kind of kid. I just researched it; I read and read. I just made it such a priority to just try and understand her, and I knew that to become physical with her, to meet her nastiness with even more nastiness in any way, wasn't right. To allow yourself to become aggressive with her would prove her right in her mind. I always knew that physical discipline was not the answer. We did have some battles over that early on, but as the years have gone on we've had less and less battles. It will always be a continuous process.

Angela: OK, well you guys are a delightful couple to spend time with and to be around, because you are always a constant reminder of what happens when you find a way to make a chaotic life really work. I really appreciate that you guys have taken the time out of your lives to talk to everybody today, and I know that this is very personal, some of the stuff that we've been talking about. On behalf of everybody, thank you. I really appreciate it and I'm hoping that you guys will come on again!

A Team Approach

In this chapter, Angela talks to Liana Palmerio-McIvor R.P., (C)OACCPP. Liana is a Registered Psychotherapist and Certified Member of the OACCPP. She has been in private practice since 1994 and enjoys working with teenagers, families and couples. Her individual work with clients is often with Bipolar, Borderline Personality Disorder, Depression and Anxiety related disorders. For more information about her, check out www.wellnesscounselling.com.

They discuss Liana's suggestions as she sheds some light on the positive role that parents can play when their child is dealing with mental illness.

This interview was first recorded June, 2013.

Angela: Why is it necessary for teens to be led by their parents? Parents can lead their children into a more positive lifestyle.

Liana: Absolutely. Parents often play a pivotal role in what path their kids are going to take. Sometimes you don't recognize these issues of mental instability until your child is well into his or her teen years. You may not have a particularly fit family or a family that focuses a lot on nutrition, but if you're encountering any kind of mental aches going on in your child, then it's really important for you to take control. A lot of parents think that when their kids hit their teens then they're old enough to make consistently good decisions and often they're not. In fact, children between the ages of twelve and seventeen enter into a phase I call the 'grey phase' where they struggle to make consistent, rational decisions a lot of time. Brain function changes during this time. The frontal lobes at this age often have lower activity and this can lead to poor control over behaviour and emotion in many teens… As well, hormones are changing, the brain is still growing and they struggle to think much about anything outside their immediate needs and wants. Parents need to help them in that grey space, remind them that sometimes, "Your wants are taking over your logic and as your parent I will be stepping in. You may not like it because you need independence, but too bad: that's my job." As well, being a role model is important—particularly with teenagers, because they are constantly watching you. If you lead a healthy life and appear happy they may try to emulate that now, or down the road. Regardless, they see what you are doing all the time, if it's positive there is no harm in that.

Angela: How important is it to show your children what a proper lifestyle choice looks like?

Liana: Teenagers are now independent at this age, in their own mind at least, and they expect you to live up to the expectations you have held up for them. The best way to parent is to be a positive role model. If you want them to exercise, get out and exercise with them. If you want them to eat healthy, make them healthy meals, show them how to make meals for themselves and eat with them as well. If you want them to go to a naturopath, go with them and try it for yourself. Being a parent is like having a 24/7 surveillance system on you: your kids watch you like a hawk. Show them how to be the best they can by modeling this behaviour.

Angela: My family and I are constantly trying to find the right balance. I have to remind myself that they look up to me to do the right things, and it's important to make sure you are showing them what that is.

Liana: Exactly! That is what I say to the families who come in and ask, "In addition to the therapy my child gets with you, how do I help my child?" And I often tell them "The first thing you do is get involved and show positive examples of healthy behaviour." They often ask this because they feel a sense of chaos and they need to be more to be involved. Often parents who have teens that are struggling with mental illness are treated quite poorly by their teen, and they feel helpless. It is not uncommon at the start of therapy with their teen, to see kids with mental illness who bully their parents.

Angela: I have seen it in families.

Liana: It is unfortunate, and often unknowingly they will bully their parents for things they want but don't necessarily need. As well, they will plead with parents not to intervene and not to help them with difficult situations because they can 'handle it.' Parents are conflicted because they are thinking, "This is my 15-year-old child. They can handle it because they are a teenager and I don't want to step on their toes or take away their independence." But often you can see them not handling a situation well, and so you can give them an opportunity to fall a little and then you intervene and say, "I'm stepping in because I am your parent." This is part of parenting.

Angela: Can you elaborate on the criteria for hospital admission?

Liana: I can't, I'm sorry. Every hospital emergency department is different. However, if you know your child has the potential to harm themselves or someone else, you need to inform the authorities and your local hospital and ask to have your teen properly assessed. You need to advocate for your child, and for yourself. If you don't do that you will not get the help that you need.

Angela: As much as we have statistics for the number of kids that are affected by mental illness, I'm guessing the actual numbers are much higher. There are so many affected in the spectrum of bipolar disorder alone.

Liana: Bipolar disorder—formerly called manic depression—is a mental illness that has severe high and low moods; changes in sleep, energy, thinking and behaviour. Unfortunately, this is a challenging disorder.

Angela: The prevalence of bipolar disorders is approximately 2.7%, but it feels like it should be much higher. It seems to be that many people have mental illness.

Liana: Well, bipolar disorder belongs to a category of disorders called mood disorders. Approximately ten percent of the US population has a mood disorder and that probably holds true for Canada as well.

Angela: What is the one common challenge parents face with bipolar disorder specifically?

Liana: I think patience is a big key. Patience with the system. Patience with your child, because he or she is not always going to present as normal, and you need to find acceptance in knowing that.

Parents need to find a place to debrief all the frustration and the anxieties they have in these circumstances. Parents also need to take care of their health, exercise and find ways to stay calm—mostly getting their heads in the game because it is a long haul. It is important for you to actively listen to your child. Active listening means engaging with your child and clarifying or validating what he or she is saying. Understand that caution is important when he or she is in manic-depressed states, because he or she may have a tendency to be impulsive, lie and exaggerate. As a parent, active listening and participation—such as asking questions and following up, is important for any teen. You must really engage and communicate to get to a place you can help him or her manage. Giving him or her context so he or she doesn't exaggerate or blow things out of proportion, is really important.

Often, their perception is a little off when they're in either state—high or low—so it's just helping them grasp reality as opposed to the irrational thinking patterns that they can dive into. Being patient and actively listening allows you to assert your parenting regularly. We talked about that before: to be on top of things with your child, to know what they are doing. Educate yourself as a parent about bipolar disorder and all the things that they could be getting into trouble with. That means you may be hyper-parenting more than for a child that does not have a mental illness, but that's not so bad. It's more work for you as a parent, but I think parents need to be highly involved in their teen's health, regardless.

Angela: My parenting style had to really change. I had to become a bigger parent in many respects in having to create context, and really talk and really understand what it was that she was going through, and to be able to lead her. I had to step back in some respects and allow her more control. That rolled off onto her siblings as well because I couldn't parent one child one way and the rest differently. A kind of give and take parenting style developed. I would say, "This is where you need to be. You need to finish school. You need to do this. You need to eat this. You need to make sure you get to the gym" and all those things. Then I would have to go to her and ask, "How do you feel?" after she did something I suggested.

Liana: Great, what you're doing in a sense, is managing her in a way to teach her how to self-care. When you have a child who has a mental illness you have to micro manage them often. Sit down with them and help them. Break down their tasks so that they don't get overwhelmed because bipolar teens get more easily overwhelmed than teens without this weight to bear. You have to help them see their challenges; like it is not a big mountain, it's a series of steps along a climb. You have to help them do that on a weekly, sometimes daily, basis.

Angela: I have been trying to give my daughter a general idea of what needs to happen, and then I go to her and ask how to help her make that happen.

Liana: It is very much based on problem solving.

Angela: To other people it looks like I'm deferring to her, not parenting. What I'm trying to do is simply push her in the right direction to get what she needs. I'm not deferring to her on what she wants. I'm giving her a framework where I am trying to draw her to a better spot. Especially during the difficult highs and lows. I can't top-down manage her because she's got to be on board, she's got to do it herself.

Liana: I think making your teen more accountable for their life by negotiating and coordinating with them on what it is that he or she needs to accomplish, is great parenting. You're saying to your daughter, "What is it that you need? How can I help you do that? You need to help me with all the pieces." This gets her involved in problem solving, as opposed to you doing everything for her. Accountability is a good word for your teaching with your daughter: you are teaching her she needs to know how to do this for herself, and she is able to see the benefits and consequences. There is a huge difference between involved parenting and enabling.

You don't want to 'over-parent' your bipolar or mentally ill child, because then you can enable their bad behavior. What you want to do, is actively parent by teaching them accountability at every turn. Sometimes they are going to fall flat on their face. You have to watch them fall a bit so they can learn, then you help them get back up, you help dust them off and then you say, "It didn't work, so how can we attack this differently, and what did we learn?" This is done by actively engaging your teen, encouraging them to come up with solutions that work for them, and that may be frustrating for them sometimes. It can especially be frustrating when you first do this process with your teen because sometimes they *want* you to take over. You need your teen to feel loved and cared for and be able to grow and make these good decisions and come up with ideas on her own. In the long run, what you create is a much more independent teen so they are wiser because of it. This is what you both want.

Angela: The trick is knowing when to step forward and when to step back. It's not always clear.

Liana: It's a bit of a dance. Patience and resilience are the keys.

Angela: It is a tough dance.

Liana: Sometimes as the parent we have to lead. We have to take over because of their state of mind, that's just the way it has to be. But most of the time your teen can lead his or her own dance: we just watch their dancing on the sideline and try to stay in step.

Angela: It takes time to get them to a place where they can actually do that on their own. It's time-consuming and frustrating, but worth it, when you see development.

Liana: Yes, because you, together, become a team. Sometimes, you have to remember that teams can have disagreements and still be successful, but there is always a coach and you are the coach, so it's important to know when to step in and when to encourage independence.

Angela: It is very team oriented.

Liana: You have to be a team because she or he can't do this on their own all the time, and enabling constantly is not a solution. Therefore, a team approach is often the best way to manage.

Angela: I like that!

Liana: Advocating for your child and working hard at being involved with your teen will create great empowerment for both of you.

Angela: Thanks so much Liana! As always, your help and insight are always appreciated.

Don't Ignore Your Gut

In this chapter, Angela interviews Liana Palmerio-McIvor, Registered Psychotherapist and Certified Member of the OACCPP. She speaks directly to parents of children with mental illness. Liana provides feedback on different parenting techniques when dealing with a child with mental illness. Her aim is to encourage parents to listen, enabling your healthcare team to refine treatment, to better support your child.

Liana has been in private practice since 1994 and enjoys working with teenagers, families and couples. Her individual work with clients is often with Bipolar, Borderline Personality Disorder, Depression and Anxiety related disorders. For more information about her, check out www.wellnesscounselling.com.

This interview was first recorded June, 2013.

Angela: If you could prevent parents from making one single, big, common mistake, what would it be?

Liana: I would say to them: first of all, listen to your gut; don't always take the word of one professional who may have misunderstood your child. You're the parent, you've raised this child, you know this child, and if you know that there's something wrong, get multiple opinions because teens are hard to put into just one box after just one meeting. "Oh don't worry, it's just anxiety" is not something you have to settle for if you know intuitively that it's more than that. Get more advice, another opinion. When the opinions start sounding repetitive, this is where you may have to land and start working on management of the condition with which your teen has been diagnosed. If your gut is telling you that your child's diagnosis isn't accurate or you want more feedback and understanding, go and get more information: you can ask for it. Go back to the hospital and ask for another psychologist's or psychiatrist's opinion. You can pay for assessments and use local resources. Or you can go to specialty clinics in the USA if you cannot get access here.

Angela: So, we all must advocate?

Liana: Yes. You have got to do what works for your teen and your family and you have to listen to your gut. If the diagnosis is something you are not comfortable with, ask. Ask and push and ask and push. If you don't push you won't always get the services you need.

Angela: I agree. The fact is, you can deal with it now or you can be in denial and deal with it when it's off the rails and it's all gone bad. What is the most common misperception, you think, that parents have of their bipolar child?

Liana: That they often feel they cannot trust their teen's behaviour all the time.

Angela: Unfortunately that does happen.

Liana: It does, because you lose trust from the repeated times they did lie to you or behaved out of character.

Angela: I can see how that happens, but you have got to reconnect and figure it out.

Liana: I think, when you finally get to a state of diagnosis and understanding of your teen's condition, a lot of trust has been broken. This is the time to rebuild and reboot: how can you work as a team if you don't trust your teen once they are properly diagnosed and receiving help?

Angela: Do you find that parents have a really hard time trusting?

Liana: Mistrust can cause crisis in the home. It can be hard to heal and to begin trusting again. If your teen, for example, steals from you or someone else while in a manic state or runs off to a party with alcohol from the family home and gets drunk and promiscuous, your trust will be stretched if not broken. It will be challenging to recover from that loss of trust, but it can be done. You can work with a therapist to rebuild it and come back to a place of forgiveness and understanding where you can distinguish between the mental illness and your child; the two are not the same.

Angela: Right, it was their illness.

Liana: Yes, in most cases it is the illness but sometimes it can just be 'normal' teen behavior.

Angela: What would you like for parents to know when dealing with a bipolar teen or child?

Liana: When this discovery happens, the focus becomes a lot about the child that is suffering with mental illness, and sometimes we forget about ourselves as people. We have to take care of ourselves as parents while we're taking care of our child, and we also have to take care of our other children.

Angela: Oh my God, yeah.

Liana: That's the hardest part as a parent. Now you're dealing with guilt and worry and the question of "How can I be everything to every child." You can get overwhelmed and stressed, so it is important to go for some of your own sessions with another therapist.

Angela: I half-jokingly say that I think, if you're a good parent of a kid that has emotional or mental challenges, you should have your own therapist, and you'll probably be medicated too. Just fasten your seatbelt and know that that's just part of the drill for a lot of people.

Liana: When your child is not well in whatever way—whether they're being bullied at school or whether they have a panic disorder, depression or a mood disorder—as a parent you personalize all of that, and how could you not? It becomes overwhelming. You worry night and day about your child, so you have to take care of yourself for sure.

Angela: I would assume quite a few people come through your door with various mental illnesses. Is Christina unusual, in that she actually followed her therapist's advice, such as embracing the fitness, nutrition and overall self-care? How unusual is that, for a client to actually do what is recommended?

Liana: Your daughter is a star when it comes to management of her disorder, in my opinion. Not every teenager will do the homework or the brainwork that is required in order to get to an improved state.

Angela: And why is that do you think?

Liana: I think teenagers get distracted by things. Immediate gratification is often the top priority for teens. I think managing health and self-care is not as interesting as other things that may pop up. I think teens with bipolar do not realize that they are in a manic state; often it just seems to them that they are having a really good time. When your teen is experiencing a low swing or depression, they often become confused and lethargic and unaware of how their behaviour affects them negatively, let alone others. The lows from depression can be debilitating. It's getting them to buy into the importance of balance overall.

The one thing I do love about working with teenagers is that often you can get them to change their behaviours and participate more in their therapy than you can with adults with a late diagnosis of mental illness. They appear more resilient, and the connection with their therapist is pivotal.

Angela: How important is routine?

Liana: A routine is really important. Teens need to understand all the things that they need to do, and process that information in small chunks so they do not feel easily overwhelmed. It also allows everyone in the family to have something to rely on when the diagnosed teen is 'in a state'. If your teen knows that, "Even though I'm in a crappy state I have to get up, I have to make this healthy lunch and I have to go and work out, because those are the things that ground me and lift me to a better state," then they will do it. I'm sure they may not always want to do it, and I'm equally sure that they will learn that if they stick to their routine, they will survive this difficult day mentally in the most healthy way possible. Routine helps your teen to get through difficult days.

Angela: How important is family support?

Liana: Family meetings in therapy, having regular support, understanding each other, having a place for you as a parent to vent, having a place for your teen to vent, having a place for your whole family to mend: all are important. Having family meetings is important so that everybody can help each other out and express how they feel about things. Doing it in a positive, calm environment is important. Getting the whole family on board is pivotal because it wouldn't be good for your teen to feel like an outsider in the family. So exercise, nutrition, psychotherapy, family meetings and routine are all very important.

Angela: Is there anything else that you can think of that can contribute to success with my bipolar teen?

Liana: Being actively involved as much as you have been, as her Mom, I am sure has enabled this process to be successful for her and for you. At the core, it's really her personality, individual resilience and dedication to her wellness that are the main reasons why she is coping as well as she has. Without you, I am sure she wouldn't be where she is, but she has that drive in her that I don't always see in others; mental illness or not.

Angela: Isn't that the truth!

Liana: There are some people that have a high pain tolerance and some people that don't; some people that are sensitive, and some people that are less so. Pain tolerance, not just in the physical sense, but in the mental pain perspective. If you keep coaching your teen, believing in them, then they can be successful. Successful attitude can be, "This sucks, but I have to deal with it and here is how I am going to do that." That's progress: logic and positive problem solving.

Angela: How much is too much encouragement? How much is too much love and communication?

Liana: There is no such thing as too much love and encouragement when you have somebody who struggles more than everybody else. So long as you're not crossing the boundary of enabling, which is letting them get out of things because they're not feeling well all the time, or doing things for your child because you feel sorry for them when they may be capable of helping themselves. That is when it becomes a problem.

Your job is to coach them, so you're on the same team but the parent is the coach. You're working together; you're problem solving together; and when they are getting tired out there in life, your job is to coach them and tell them to get up and keep going. That is sometimes all you can do: you don't let your teen quit, because they can't. When they can't get up, you as a parent help them get up. You will instinctively know when they have had too much. Again, we come back to listening to your gut. I have a friend who has an Asperger's child and the parent used to be in school all the time and go to classes with the child and sometimes the child would have outbursts in class. They finally got him ECE support workers who are with him through the day and it has been such a great support to both her son and to her. Now she can pop into the school to say "Hi." She can now supervise and coach her son with the support she needed. Great parents of children with extra challenges or mental illness are often coaching and teaching, not always saving or enabling. It feels better, especially when all the supports are in place.

Angela: What would you say to people that don't believe in mental illness? They say the child is overindulged and spoiled?

Liana: So what you're asking me is, why other people have said to you, "It's not bipolar, maybe it's something else?"

Angela: That is constant. They say, "I think it's all in your head, I think it was a misdiagnosis. She's been overindulged and she is spoiled and you're participating in it."

Liana: A lot of people attach so much stigma to mental illness. Some people make this kind of judgmental statements because they feel somehow personally affected by what you're doing for your child and they may also be afraid of the label. You'd have to ask yourself why they are so affected by this diagnosis. I think you need to say to them, "You know, there are people out there that are capable and qualified to make this diagnosis, and we've had more than one person weigh in on this diagnosis." The clear fact is, if medication changes my child's state into a more grounded, positive or better place then there was definitely something 'off' for my child that medication could address. Therefore, a diagnosis is valid.

Angela: Thank you, that's a great way to explain it.

Liana: There is no way that a child can normally go from a perky, sweet, goal oriented person to a sobbing, depressed, self-sabotaging personality. These types of changes in your child's mood are often associated with what is going on in their brain chemistry.

Angela: Is there anything that I haven't covered that you think would be helpful for the parents out there?

Liana: Just what I mentioned earlier: that the resources for mental health remain a challenge so you need to recognize that the squeaky wheel gets the grease.

Angela: I still can't believe how uninformed I was. There are no lessons; there are no schools; no intensive therapy sessions for parents. The parents in every case need to do some of the research and talk to people like yourself who have experience in dealing with mental illness.

Liana: It's also important for people with mental illness to have goals and not see themselves as ill. Parents play a vital role in that, but also the child plays a vital role. They need to be actively engaging with their therapist, to see this is a condition that they can learn to manage and cope with and know that they do not have to be dragged down by it.

Angela: Christina was quite stable for probably 20 months or so. There was some fluctuation, of course, but pretty good stability. Then all of a sudden a crash... What happened?

Liana: While I can't comment on specifics, I can say that sometimes brain chemistry can change, which can affect how someone responds to a particular medication or combination of medications.

Parents need to be prepared for this and to come back to the core principles of understanding and support for your child, and of course to stay engaged with your healthcare team, which can include a family doctor or a psychiatrist.

Angela: Thank you so much, Liana, for the interview. You have helped a lot of parents today.

Additional Resources

Angela and her guests have put together a collection of resources to help parents of challenging children. It includes nutrition and exercise advice, checklists and other useful tips and information.

You can get a copy by visiting

http://www.dftok.com/bonus-page

Shame Is Only A Perception

In this chapter, we speak with Wendy, a psychotherapist, and mother of a young woman diagnosed with Bipolar Disorder. Wendy holds postgraduate degrees in psychology and education, and is currently completing her doctorate in psychology. She brings thirty years of experience in counselling, consulting and training. Wendy utilizes her expert knowledge to help us take the positive from one's situation, no matter what your circumstance is.

This interview was first recorded June, 2013.

Angela: Please describe the two or three most effective things you can do to support your child diagnosed with Bipolar Disorder.

Wendy: What comes to mind—and this is sort of an umbrella concept I guess—is recognizing that your child is not going to be like you. I think as parents we tend to assume that our children will be like "mini-me's" to some degree, and usually our children are. Between the effects of nature, nurture, genetics and socialization, when we raise our children we can generally know what to expect. We can say "Oh yeah, I was like that as a kid," or, "her Dad did that as a kid," or, "I did that at that age."

We live, to a varying degree, a similar experience, so, whether it is my sister or me, we can usually relate. And if not, we are still able to be open and comfortable confiding in each other. The issue is that not many people discuss or even talk about mental illness, so when one's child experiences a diagnosis it can really alter a parent's thoughts and feelings about parenthood.

For me, it was a really important place to start and (especially once you have a diagnosis) to acknowledge that you are parenting a child that you don't always understand, one that doesn't always make sense to you. For me it was a really important starting point to acquire a diagnosis, to be able to understand. It's natural for parents to think, "I'm not comfortable with this behaviour, I never did this…, my husband never did this…"

It's really important to embrace the gift that you're given. You need to believe that there is some purpose for you. I tend to think that things happen for a reason, that we are meant to be together and it's all for something better. This may not be an easy journey, but it's meaningful. People need to begin this process as positive instead of negative; see it as an opportunity and a gift that has great potential, and that it truly is meaningful.

Angela: If you could prevent parents from making one common, single, big mistake, what would it be?

Wendy: What comes to mind is to focus on the person, not just the illness. There is a great quote that I am having difficulty recalling right now, but it goes something like this… "It's not so important what illness a person has, but what person has the illness." People are more than their diagnosis: this is essential and to be put first.

What I have seen happen is that people's lives can get really bogged down once they get a diagnosis because everyone then begins saying, "Oh well, you're bipolar," "You did that because you are bipolar," "I won't even talk to you about this because you are bipolar." But, hold on: what I want you to say is, "I'm a person." It can become a nice, neat excuse, and becomes a way of blaming as well as a way of avoiding because everything gets put in the box. It can even actually cause problems; the diagnosis becomes an issue in itself. Even as a parent, you begin just seeing the diagnosis. "She's doing this because she's bipolar"… instead of, "maybe she's just not eating well," "maybe she's tired," "maybe that's just who she is." Everything isn't because she's bipolar.

Angela: What would you say is the most common misperception?

Wendy: I remember struggling with this. I was told by my daughter's doctor, and she told it to both of us actually, in the same session: **"You do not have to apologize."** It was good for me to hear that, and it was good for her to hear it. "It wasn't you, it was your illness. You don't have to apologize for your illness." If I had an epileptic seizure while I'm sitting here (I'm not epileptic, but let's say I was) and let's say I have a seizure… how do I owe you an apology? It's not pleasant for you, you are not going to enjoy it, but do I owe you an apology? I do take responsibility, after my seizure. I will fix the chair if appropriate. I will fix you a fresh cup of tea. I will apologize—most likely anyway—because I'm polite and I want to make you feel comfortable, but I do not feel **shame**.

Socially and behaviorally, you have to take responsibility. You can't just be a bull in a china shop and say "I'm sick - and it's not my fault…" We don't want people saying that. You have to live your life, warts and all. You have to be responsible. But at a deeper level, it looks at the issue of shame. "There is something profoundly not OK with me because I threw a table at my mother. What kind of a person would do that?" Well, a person having a rage attack because they are sick, just like that person was having a seizure. What kind of person would fall out of their chair and kick their friend? The kind of person that is having a seizure. It doesn't mean that they can do whatever they want because they are bipolar: it's not that either. There are certainly some responsibilities there, but I think that is a really important distinction to understand.

Angela: What are the top three tell-tale signs that parents should be looking for?

Wendy: I ran an anger management program before I became a psychotherapist for individuals with severe behavioral problems. So I'm pretty skilled at behaviour management, and when it comes to children and difficult behaviors I'm probably as skilled as anybody. And I was a total failure with my own daughter. I mean, a total failure. I remember the day a girlfriend said to me "Wendy why don't you try rewarding positive behaviours and ignoring the other behaviour?" And I just looked at her and said to myself "Are you nuts? Do you have any idea how hard I work at this?" She was only in Grade 1 or 2 when I looked at her and thought, "there is something wrong, like there is _really_ something wrong."

Social learning is pretty consistent. I mean I have worked with some pretty difficult individuals, and it didn't matter what I did for her: it just didn't seem to work. She was six, and it took until she was twenty-eight years old before I got a diagnosis. We went to lots of doctors and lots of therapists, and it's sad to say no one could figure out what it was for all those decades, which is pretty horrible, but her diagnosis didn't even exist back then. So when looking back, that would be my first clue as a parent: when you're observing that normal rewards or consequences don't work. I was dealing with something that is not typical and now we can see that she couldn't control it.

When I am screening people for bipolar, I often encourage them to keep a calendar to track two things: really bad events and really good events. So, you have really good events: the kid just got to be the lead in the school play, or say, tomorrow is her birthday. Then you have really bad events: she fell and broke her arm, or didn't get the lead in the play. Track those events and then track moods up and down. What happens is, over time if you are bipolar, the mood won't match the events. Moods will fluctuate in a cycle, like perhaps every three weeks moods cycle up, and then they cycle down every three weeks. If I'm in a down cycle and I win the lottery it won't even affect the mood I'm in. In other words, the cycle will not correlate with a good or bad event. If something wonderful happens, you've just won the lottery and you're depressed then your brain chemistry doesn't match up. Your brain chemistry doesn't care if it's your birthday and you just got a pony, so the calendar tracking is a great tool, and if you do that for about six months it's a valuable tool.

Angela: What would be the top three strategies for parents with children who have a mental illness?

Wendy: Order, as opposed to chaos, is really important. Order is really important for all of us, but particularly important for someone struggling emotionally or who is emotionally sensitive, or in this case bipolar. Today, it's not normal to have order. Chaotic households are so normal these days. Everybody is working extra hours and working odd shifts; everyone is under stress, and they are bringing work home with them: we come to accept that as the norm. It's really an act of rebellion to parent in a way that's abnormal; which is calm, orderly, and grounded; with some space in between activities; with some space in between expectations.

You can't continue to be the driven 'Type A' personality… It's fabulous for the parent to slow down as well, but it is difficult to do, and it is a bit of an act of rebellion. We feel abnormal if we are not doing something every evening, but with kids like this, instead we should sit and talk, have a leisurely dinner, or play a board game.

The second thing would be setting realistic expectations and dealing with your own expectations for your children, which are often expectations based on our own needs. We need to learn to figure out what is a healthy expectation for the child, as opposed to your own needs and wishes. It actually is a really lovely, sensitive, parenting technique to tune into your kids and ask, "What are you thinking? What are you feeling?" It's exhausting, which is why I wouldn't say every parent should do this, but you have to if you have a sensitive child that needs that. If they have needs and moods that change day to day, you need to know that. It's like, if you're recovering from a broken ankle, you need to know how much weight you can bear on it; how long you can walk on it today. You're not just going to get up and run a marathon.

The third strategy would be to look after yourself, because you are the foundation of this support system. If the foundation crumbles, the rest of the building crumbles as well, so self-care is really critical to your ability to give the support.

Angela: What do you see as the greatest challenge the bipolar person faces?

Wendy: Obviously, the greatest challenge is their illness. It is the quantity of time managing it. What comes close behind that is the price they pay. They have to focus on their illness and the consequences of their illness, instead of managing other things. There can often be gaps in normal development, age-appropriate, developmental skills. They may be academic, they may be social, they may be social emotional. All through childhood, children are learning and growing at a rapid pace. One requires their brain to develop, but the bipolar brain is occupied by other things. There are some people diagnosed with bipolar that despite their age—whether late twenties, early thirties or later—don't develop some of the skills that they should have learned as a teenager but didn't. There are things that are missing and that just basically pass them by. The good news is that once the brain is stable, we can learn developmental tasks and pick them up really quickly as we get older. You can learn it much more quickly when you're ready to learn. It's important to look at those ages and stages and evaluate what may have been neglected or not learned.

Another major challenge is self-esteem. This goes back to the whole theme of shame associated with the diagnosis: "I did bad things, I acted inappropriately therefore I must be a bad person." As an example, I may not have a large following in my practice of bipolar patients, but I certainly have many patients that are ADD, ADHD or have learning disabilities. Every person that I've ever met with any of those things has self-esteem issues: they all believe that they are stupid. It's horrible. That's what happens. We get messages in the brain when we are young, and everything is black and white. If you are doing something as a child that is bad, you begin to believe that **you** are bad. The core of self-esteem is established in childhood, so I believe that everyone should do self-esteem work: work very actively on correcting those negative core beliefs while also giving moral and emotional support.

Angela: Is there anything else that you would like to say before we conclude our interview together?

Wendy: We all have strengths and weaknesses - get out there and use your strengths! Everybody has weaknesses and problems. There is no such thing as a perfectly balanced human being that doesn't have some problems, some issue, whether it's physical, mental, or emotional—never! There is a tendency to focus on our weaknesses. First thing in the morning, you wake up thinking about 'the problem'. We just continue to zoom in on 'the problem,' and this sets your tone (or you could call it your emotional tone) for the rest of the day. It's kind of like waking up negative and worried because, "I'm not perfect."

I'm not saying we shouldn't address our weaknesses or our issues, but we shouldn't focus only on them. We really need to focus on our strengths. We all have gifts, and you should be able to get up and say, "This is my gift, and today I'm going to soar and be joyful. I'm going to use it and be full of love for myself, as I have this gift." Once again, I'm not saying that you should ignore it, but it shouldn't be the focus. If we raise our children knowing that, it really frees them to live in a way that makes them happy.

Contributing And Staying Connected

In this chapter we talk to Lynn, a woman who deals with mental illness day-to-day and describes to us different ways that she keeps a balanced life while also staying connected to people in the community.

Lynn, once in the highly competitive and high pressure world of academia, now lives her life near the water in Southern Ontario, volunteering in her community for many festivals and celebrations. She is very involved volunteering with the library programs, and as of this year is now responsible for their public garden project.

Lynn is a wonderful example of how people who struggle with mental illness can still contribute to our community in great ways.

This interview was first recorded August, 2013.

Angela: I am here with Lynn who has been kind enough to join us for an interview. I wanted to talk to Lynn because she has had a bipolar diagnosis at one point in her life and has moved on through it. We want to look into how to live a balanced life while dealing with a mental illness, and get a glimpse into what her life looks like. She does a lot of volunteer work and I would like to talk about where her life has taken her.

Hi Lynn, welcome. Tell me about your voluntary activities now, and what your life looks like generally.

Lynn: In the past there were periods of time in depression and extreme agitation when I wasn't able to do anything. I wasn't able to walk through hallways, out the front door, or be able to communicate at all. I was very socially frightened. Since emerging from that period, I have been pushing myself to go further and further. I participate in the community, which is what I used to do when I was working full-time in a corporation.

What I want to mention to individuals that are looking at a bipolar diagnosis, or parents of bipolar children, is that life takes a lot of unexpected turns. A diagnosis of bipolar is frustrating and can devastate an individual and their immediate family and friends. It is a process of understanding that certain chemicals are working differently in your body. You need to go through a re-collaboration or adjustment. I found that the work life I had, the pace of life that I had in the corporate environment, was too challenging for me. It left me fighting for self-worth when I wasn't able to work at my job anymore. I have an ongoing relationship with my physicians, which has helped me maintain a better balance in my life. The biggest thing I had to learn was to recognize that I have to let go of concerns and thoughts that were negative and stalked me.

Everybody has worries. Everybody has hopes and dreams for the future. But when those things began to drive my day-to-day life beyond my capacity to cope, I had to let them go. The medication that I was prescribed almost forces me to let go. I'm not able to retain the kind of ambitious plans that I used to entertain when I was working all the time. When you're in a collective environment of great thinkers and great achievers, you want to keep pace with them and set goals for yourself that may or may not be achievable. They are not things that I can strive for on a day-to-day basis and end it happily, so I have settled for a happier life.

Angela: Good for you! So what does that happier life entail for you?

Lynn: Basically, I have to push myself beyond the perimeters of what I would like to do on a day-to-day basis. That means that I have to stay involved in the community. I have always done a lot of voluntary work, and that has continued. The community-based volunteer work keeps me active socially and communicating with a variety of people: high achievers, wealthy people, individuals that are struggling on Ontario works, or under the Ontario disability program.

I've volunteered in a few food banks; I've volunteered at the library; I work on community festivals; I help friends when they are going through struggles with their own mental and physical challenges. I walk a few dogs in my community, and that's been very helpful for me because it keeps me physically active and it keeps me in-line and on a schedule.

I guess the instinct is to evaluate one's success on an economic scale, or on an accomplishment scale or on a material scale, but I now evaluate the enjoyment of life instead of its accomplishments, which is very important for those with mental illness.

Angela: What is the most rewarding, and why?

Lynn: I guess all of them are rewarding in different ways. I really enjoy going to the food bank and community centre. It's a chance to interact with people there that are friendly and social. It feels like home. There are always ways to contribute and have my contribution appreciated. The library is another environment I find great. It's an environment open to the public, and I'm surrounded by books, magazines, DVDs and music. Many people come in and enjoy learning for the first time. It's an exciting environment; I enjoy it.

Angela: Yeah you strike me as someone who truly relates to academic surroundings and art.

Lynn: I liked learning from the time I was a little kid, I was a great reader, and my mother and father are very wise and successful. I don't think I'm academic in the sense of wanting to study everything, but academic in the sense of, "let's look at this to evaluate it and analyze it." I don't want to always just be reactive; I like to think things all the way through.

Angela: Why does being active in your community help you feel grounded?

Lynn: It gives me a sense of self-worth and it gives me a sense of accomplishment. After my work experience with the university, I was very interested in experiential learning and fascinated with a world that's so torn economically, between those that have, and those that have not and come from different countries. I'm interested in how people learn to live together. That's the kind of lifestyle I have now: it allows me talk to, and be friends with, people who have handicaps, or physical or mental disorders. I also get to meet individuals that have accomplished a lot, worked very hard for it, and have a lot of material things.

Angela: You're just that kind of person then? One who goes out of their way for others?

Lynn: I'll see people on the street holding up signs that were mocking the community because nobody would really see them. I see them and acknowledge them with a smile, and they would nod and smile at me because nobody would read their sign.

Angela: I think that anyone who has been through any of the stuff that you, or my daughter have been through…it makes you a lot more tuned into people, and a lot more empathetic. Would you agree with that?

Lynn: Yes, sometimes too much!

Angela: Yes, I see that in both of you.

Lynn: If you have mental health issues, you get so close to the edge and fall, and don't know how to get back. Your only hope is that you get back. Your eyes can be opened to many, many things. You can see far beyond the perimeters of what most people can see. In getting better, you are really cautious about how far and how fast you can go.

Angela: I know my daughter can be very sensitive to people's energies. My daughter is so much more intuitive. She reads people's expression like no one I have known. When my daughter walks into a social environment, she can read the room. Sometimes she will avoid people's eye contact to avoid feeling overwhelmed, depending on how she's feeling that day. Have you ever had that?

Lynn: Yes.

Angela: How do you protect yourself?

Lynn: There were periods of time when I was in a real awareness stage, and I couldn't walk through crowds. I would pick up too much energy. I used to be afraid at times, but you must remember not to let these types of things bring you down.

I was afraid, sometimes, that I would absorb too much of people's pain, whether psychic, emotional or physical pain. In the process of sympathetic communication I tend to mimic or copy what the other person is feeling. You start to feel it in your body, and there are times I was really sensitive to that and that I was holding on to too much.

When you talked about your daughter avoiding eye contact when she is in a bad mental state, it is for the same reason autistic people avoid it. Sometimes it's just too much to deal with.

They avoid eye contact because they're afraid of feeling too much. I could look at people's eyes and feel like I was swallowed, or that I'd just fallen right into them and that I would feel so sensitively linked to them. Sometimes it was like the sound of nails being dragged on a chalkboard, you know? You cringe, not knowing how to manage this. It can be frightening, really sad, and very exciting, very enlightening.

I belong on this path in life, and I have to assert myself and push myself along that path. It's like God chooses to reveal Himself at certain times. That doesn't mean He wants to make us all a witness every day. We all have insights every day, and moments that are filled with greatness. It's part of who I am, and what I've learned to accept is that I can't predict what's going to happen every day. I have to balance myself at those times when I feel that I'm being pressured. I'm careful about how close I get to people, how involved I get with them. I think parents of children that are in that situation carry an extra measure of worry because they have a reason to be afraid that their child will not be able to set boundaries; that they are not protected enough.

Angela: Things have been written about people with the diagnosis of bipolar or some other mental illness, who have been taken advantage of because the boundaries are not clearly set in their heads. Can you speak to that a little bit for me?

Lynn: Yeah, I think that can happen very regularly. They run the risk of meeting the wrong people or choosing the wrong friends; they run the risk of criminal problems; they run the risk of getting into a hospital and having doctors there that aren't listening to them, or aren't taking them seriously.

Angela: You and I had a conversation one night. I asked what you thought may have been happening with today's youth with the increase mental illness generally. You said it was based on electronics interfering with our brains. Could you elaborate more, because it was a really interesting conversation?

Lynn: Every child today is being traumatized to some extent by their own environment, knowing too early what it's like to go through poverty, war, job loss and everything in between. Kids are being pushed to accept a never-ending upgrade of computer technology and telecommunication.

Angela: So there is no balance, right? We've lost grounding?

Lynn: We've moved away too far from the agricultural community where people sat around the farm table to have a meal with their family. We all might sit around the table and have a meal, but it's different now. You need to know family means something, friends mean something, so does your own sense of self. You need to know you are going to get through it.

Angela: OK, Lynn, it's always interesting having a conversation with you. Thank you so much for joining us, I really appreciate it. I'm hoping that we can do this again sometime.

A Quick Fix Is Just A Quick Fix

In this chapter, we dive into the life journey of Jennifer Bitner, and her experiences dealing with high level anxiety. This is a moving story of a young woman trying to get help in a society where mental health is not discussed. Jennifer offers great insight into how we can start taking control of our mental health through some lifestyle changes.

This interview was first recorded July, 2013.

Angela: I'm sitting here with Jennifer Bitner. Jennifer is a dynamic, multi-talented, and very successful young woman. Many people suffer from all different kinds of anxiety. I thank you for coming forward to share your story with the parents listening. Anxiety is a huge challenge and can show up in early childhood. Please tell us a little about your story.

Jennifer: I went to Western University, where I acquired my degree in sociology. Once I graduated, I got a cross-disciplinary degree with an area of concentration focusing on youth at risk. One thing I took with me from school was extra weight. When I got to university without my Mom's home cooking, I gained about forty pounds.

Following graduation, I was in this post-grad depression, and I had no idea what I wanted to do with my life. My cousin gave me a business card of the general manager at a Fitness Club and told me it would be a good, dynamic place to work.

I applied at the Fitness Club. My thoughts were, "working out never came easy to me and I never worked out before, and I don't know anything about fitness. I think I might want to be a teacher, so what if I can go work in their child minding department while I try to figure out if I can go to teachers college?"

I went to the Fitness Club. The General Manager immediately offered me the sales position. Within the first three months I was cramming with every single book I could find about fitness, because I was selling fitness and personal training but I didn't know anything about it. I learned everything I could learn and got myself a personal trainer to lose the university weight and to learn about what I was selling.

I turned out to be the second highest salesperson in the country that year and was nominated as membership consultant of the year. I went on to become a general manager at the age of twenty-three. I was really young, but I worked really hard at what I did. I had a passion for being successful but the whole fitness part of it never came easy to me. I was passionate about being successful and that happened to be the industry that I was in. I hired a trainer, because I knew that I wasn't motivated enough to work out on my own. I had to hire a nutritionist to help me with my food, because I didn't know how to eat properly nor was I motivated to eat properly.

Angela: How old are you now?

Jennifer: I'll be thirty years old next month.

Angela: You've struggled and been challenged with some stuff. Can you talk a little bit about it?

Jennifer: I've been with the company eight years, and I have been a general manager for six years now, and I love teaching people about fitness. It's hard for me to actually stay motivated to do what I have to do, but I understand why I have to work out and eat healthy. So, it's not something that I'm addicted to: it's something that I have to do. I believe the majority of the population can relate to that.

The reason that I have to do it comes from a lifelong block: I am someone who deals with severe anxiety. It was only seven years ago that I was struck with anxiety and panic attacks. In the last year, I was able to unlock a series of repressed memories that were causing me to become anxious and panic.

My whole life I lived without the panic attacks, but I still lived with some shame. I didn't realize the pain these repressed memories and feelings were causing, which leads me to today and something that happened an hour before I got to your house, which was probably why I was late. So it's very neat that we're having this conversation today.

My panic and anxiety started about seven years ago. I was with my boyfriend. We were in the car and we had just left Square One shopping centre. I had eaten Taco Bell. Fast food didn't sit well, because I already put on weight from the bad food that I ate throughout school. I was just starting on this health kick, when I had this fast food and my body didn't agree with it. I'm sitting in the car, bumper to bumper traffic on Burnhamthorpe; we were sitting at these stop lights and all of a sudden I'm like, "I have to go to the bathroom! I have got to go like right now!" He's like, "What do you want me to do? Where am I going to stop? Where am I going to go?" And I'm like, "I have to get out of this car!"

I couldn't breathe. I broke out into a full sweat. The first ever panic attack I had was in the car! We finally made it to a Pizza Pizza. I ran out, got to the bathroom. All I was thinking was, "Life is ok, for now." I started crying and I'm like, "Oh my gosh, what was that? What was that panic?" I never felt that before. I didn't know it was a panic attack. I had never heard of panic or anxiety in my life. We got to my boyfriend's house, and I was going to the bathroom every fifteen minutes; just feeling sick, gross and embarrassed. I was outright ashamed and humiliated that this had happened.

From that one moment, fast forward to the next seven years of my life, and I am completely traumatized by cars and brake lights. Every single time I see a brake light, it reminds me of that event: being in that car, being stuck and having to go to the bathroom. It got so bad that every time I would see brake lights, I would have a full anxiety or panic attack, thinking that I was stuck in the car and couldn't get to a bathroom. Anywhere that I went for the next seven years, if I saw brake lights, I would have a panic attack. We would go out to dinner, stop at a stoplight on the way and I would start having anxiety. Then my body would recreate the sensation of having to go to the bathroom. I spent the next seven years thinking I had to go to the bathroom, like a hundred times a day, I was having three, four or five panic attacks a day, and anxiety constantly.

My whole body was in crisis mode—literally in fight or flight mode—all day long, for seven years. The first year, back tracking to when it first happened, I didn't tell a single soul. I was the kind of person that perfection and living as a perfectionist was very important to me. I've been in pageants. I was very proper, and I had held onto things that had happened in my previous relationships as skeletons in my closet which I only kept to myself and didn't tell anybody. I always wanted to live in this very "I'm perfect" world. I spent the first year telling people that I was just car sick, and that's why I always had to pull over. It was finally about a year into my relationship and my boyfriend says "I'm very concerned about you, I believe you have an eating disorder and I'm very concerned for you because you always have to throw up." I was too ashamed to say "It's because I have to go to the bathroom so I have to pull over all the time." That's when I realized, "Oh shoot, I'd better tell somebody." I finally told him that, "It's not throwing up; in fact I feel like I have to go to the bathroom all the time, and I don't know why."

I finally went to my doctor. She said, "Maybe you just have an anxiety disorder." I'm like, "What's an anxiety disorder?" She said, "Well let me just recommend you to the adult mental health clinic." I'm like, "You've got to be kidding me, if you think I'm going to a mental health clinic. Perfect Jennifer, top in the sales of my company, walk into a place called the adult mental health clinic? Are you kidding?" But I'm also like, "I can't live like this anymore so I have to do something."

I walked into this clinic for the first time, and I had my hair in front of my face. I tried to cover up who I was. I looked in the window before I even walked in, to see if I knew anyone, because I was like, "mental health? I am not going to a place called mental health."

I finally met my counsellor, who I called Dr. Jane. I don't even think she was a doctor, but I called her Dr. Jane anyways. She tried to coach me through this. The psychiatrist put me on Paxil, 25 mg a day, and I started this medication to try to ease the anxiety that I was constantly having. I became so addicted to it that if I didn't have the medication at the exact same time every single day I would have major withdrawal symptoms. I would have headaches and I'd feel sick to my stomach.

Angela: Do you think that was a part of the anxiety?

Jennifer: I have no idea, but I know that when I was on that medication life was not good.

I took it for a year. I actually was hiding a lot of the stuff from doctors because I was too ashamed to tell them what actually was happening. They'd say, "Have you ever X, Y and Z?" and I'd be like, "Nope." Meanwhile I had, but I didn't want to tell the counsellor that because I was ashamed. I had all the shame inside me, and I didn't know why I was ashamed. I just was.

Medication didn't work, but I tried to live my life and it progressively started getting worse.

Say I went to a friend's apartment, and it's two bedroom, one bathroom. The second someone walked into that bathroom, I had a full blown panic attack because, "What if I have to go? Now you're in it. Now I can't get in there. I can't go to the bathroom. You're in the bathroom." I'd knock on the door, and I'd be like, "You need to get out. You need to get out. I have to go. I have to go."

My body would recreate the sensation of needing to go, and it would recreate the exact sensation I had when I had that Taco Bell incident and I was sitting in that car. That sensation would be recreated seven times a day, any time where I wasn't close or freely able to go to a bathroom.

I started getting out of family functions. We'd go to my (now) husband's family's house, and I would fake food poisoning. I would fake the 'flu. I would fake everything. I had to get myself out of their house because I'd start having anxiety attacks. I would look at where the bathroom was and I'd be like, "This is way too close to everyone. They're going to all hear me in there." So then I started to reflect. This isn't just from that one Taco Bell incident. When I think back to my university years, I actually was like this for the entire three years I was in university. I had this phobia or obsession with bathrooms. Every single time I had to go to the bathroom, I was worried that people would hear me, so I would run the water; I'd flush the toilet; I brought a stereo into my bathroom in my residence so I could have music playing all the time, 24 hours a day. Just so when I went to the bathroom, no one could hear me.

It started getting worse and worse in university. I started becoming obsessed with certain times of the day. So I'd sit in a class, but as soon as the clock hit 10:20 a.m., my stomach instantly started making the sensation that I had to go to the bathroom. I would get out of my class, I'd go to the bathroom and I wouldn't return. I had to drop one of my criminology classes on Tuesdays and Thursday's because it was at 10 a.m. and at 10.20 a.m. my body would recreate the sensation of having to go to the bathroom. That's why I kept it a secret for so long, because I was such a girly girl and I was such a catholic girl; there is a set of certain values that makes you feel ashamed of certain things.

The three years I was in university, I was obsessed with bathrooms. I was obsessed with the thought of people hearing me go to the bathroom and the social embarrassment that would have come along with people hearing me go to the bathroom.

So, if my first panic attack wasn't until *after* University, then why could I remember being so anxious about bathrooms even *during* university? This is what I was able to uncover just recently during a meditation session. I realized for all these years, I was actually living in the shame, embarrassment and guilt from an incident that happened when I was four. A little four year old girl, on a school bus. I had to "go pee" so badly, and at that age I think it's quite common for little kids to need to go at inopportune times. I remember vividly the bus driver screaming at me to sit down. I wasn't allowed to get up and go. So… I had no choice. I had to go. Right there, on the bus. So I did. She yelled at me, scolded me, and the other kids laughed. Once I brought this memory up to the conscious level, I was finally able to deal with it. I had been hiding the shame my whole life. Didn't even tell my counsellors or my Mom. I could now see how I brought this phobia and fear with me throughout my years, through university, then into my adult life. I also realized how that moment in the car after Taco Bell triggered that memory from when I was stuck on the school bus when I was four, which led to years of further panic and anxiety.

I never shared with anyone until now, because I'm starting to realize how my mind has created this whole phobia. Medication was not working; counselling was not working. So I tried getting myself into more natural ways of therapy. I decided that if the medication is not working…the counselling is not working…OK, let's try something else.

It's funny because I had no resources; nobody talks about mental disorders or mental illnesses, so nobody I knew had ever suffered from what I suffered from. No one else talked about it, so I didn't talk about it. I suffered in silence for years. I couldn't do anything, couldn't go anywhere, didn't go on trips, and definitely couldn't go on road trips. We couldn't go anywhere because I'd get in the car and I'd have a panic attack as soon as we got in the car. I began to refuse to live in such an isolated manner that prevented me from living my life to the fullest.

I Googled anxiety disorder and came across the Panic Away program. I downloaded it, and it came with a guarantee, so I printed it off, did the program. The program changed my life. It was all about the lifestyle changes that need to be made: getting support, giving meaning to the anxiety and understanding what your body is going through. You need to understand what's happening in your mind. Then progressing lifestyle changes, food, hydration and working out.

I did this program while I was away in Australia, which gave me time to really focus on these lifestyle changes. Six months later, I went back to work. Within three weeks of being at work, the stress came back; the lifestyle changes went to the side. I stopped working out, stopped doing all that stuff, and bam! The anxiety came back ten times worse. Someone said "Why don't you try hypnotherapy? Why don't they hypnotize you, so that you get over this situation?"

So I decided to try hypnotherapy. Two thousand dollars and two years later, I couldn't get over this anxiety. "That's not working, so let's try something else." I finished with hypnotherapy but they had introduced me to NLP, or Neuro Linguistic Programming.

My Mom then suggested I try Reiki. I wasn't open minded to Reiki because I wasn't really open minded to anything holistic, but at this point I wanted to give this a go. So I did the Reiki. I did Reiki for about six months and then I was feeling so much more relaxed, so much better. I thought, "this is good." My mind started becoming clear. I stopped having anxiety and I stopped having panic attacks.

I started seeing a naturopath. The naturopath put me on a diet for eight weeks: Vitamin D, no gluten and no dairy for eight full weeks. Not only did I lose all my weight, but my brain was so clear. I had no anxiety, no panic attacks. I started working out three times a week. I started craving working out. It was a crazy turnaround, this past year. I went through all the natural ways. I changed the diet, started liking working out and I felt amazing. The anxiety started subsiding, it started going away. Now, I realize why we should exercise. Now, I realize why we should eat properly. If we don't, there are bad effects on the body and mind.

You are what you eat, and that couldn't be more true. If you're consistently eating 'unclean' food every single day; every single day, your moods will be altered. For people out there that are saying "I will do anything to get through these mood disorders," then change your diet. Just change your food: that will have such an effect. Also exercise. Exercise three times a week. Choose the right foods and feel the difference in your mood. You'll hear this everywhere.

It's so simple but there are so many different things that are put on the market: cleanses, diets that people want to buy into because they think if they do that for seven days then they are cured and can go back to the way they were. No! If you eat properly, you have to do it again for the next day to be good for the day after that.

I've gone through every practitioner under the sun. Why? Because I am the queen of a quick fix. I kept going the easy route, and every single time it led me back to the same thing. Which is eating properly, exercising to release the stress and release the endorphins. Then you can think clearly and your body will start healing itself. The only way you can allow your body to naturally heal itself is by giving your body what it needs: water, calmness, some meditation, and the right foods. Go join a gym; great money invested. Get a personal trainer; great money invested. Go see a holistic nutritionist who can give you a prescription for food, not medicine, because food is medicine.

The people who mentally need to get healthier have nowhere to turn. There are not many resources available. That's when I came up with My Mind Fitness. Mind fitness is as important as physical fitness. You cannot take on anything if you are not fit, or in a healthy place mentally, to be able to make those changes. The power of thought is everything. Your thoughts move your life. You will either talk yourself out of something or talk yourself into something. Direct your time and invest it back into things that are going to be healthy and contribute positively towards eating better, exercise, and taking a half hour to do meditation.

You have twenty-four hours in a day. It's how you use those hours that makes you who you are.

Mental health is something that nobody should suffer with in silence, because so many people go through it. I had hidden a lot of the effects that had come with my anxiety. When you have something mentally going on, you need to be as open and honest as possible with everything you're going through. It is so hard to do those four concepts; to do the sleep, stress control, nutrition and movement. If you're going to put money into anything, put money into one of those four modalities that are going to help you.

Don't put money into figuring out how to get rid of this temporarily. Don't do that. Do something that will teach you how to properly do those four things, until you can do it on your own, then you can wean yourself off the trainer, or you can wean yourself off your nutritionist.

What was it like for our ancestors before all the stress, technology, jobs, mass consumption and the mass production? What was it like when it was the way it was supposed to be? The way we're supposed to be born? That's what you have to concentrate on. That would be my recommendation.

Angela: Thank you so much, thank you so much for sharing with us today Jennifer, your advice is great. Stick to the four things in our lives that control our mental state: stress control, sleep, exercise and food. It was wonderful to hear from someone who knows from firsthand experience.

Conclusion

Hopefully, after reading this book, parents whose children are affected by mental illness feel a little less isolated. I'm hoping that those who feel at wit's end might find a little peace of mind. I'm hoping that everyone takes away a little more insight into the trials and tribulations that come with raising a challenging child.

We have been lucky to have interviewed a range of people who are affected with, or are affected by, mental illness. From those (now, adult) children who suffer, to professionals that treat them, we have heard how difficult it can be. However, there is hope. I want parents to find some solace, some peace, in knowing that what they deal with daily is experienced by many parents. The more we learn, the more we can help coach our children and be the support system they deserve.

This effort originally began back in early 2012, when I thought I was going to write a book about the experience I had with raising Christina. After figuring out that writing a book was not nearly as easy as I thought, and having interviewed people for the book, I realized that there could be strength from the actual interviews and not just a retelling of a story in book form. I began this project with the thought that no parent should feel as isolated and unprepared as I was.

Unfortunately, there have been quite a few 'edits' within this project.

Some, after having spoken their mind plainly, have had to pull back on their truth for fear of repercussions, either personally or professionally. Some of what was truly compelling in the interview process has been softened, and in some cases, eliminated for fear of reprisal… It seems it is one thing to have a side-bar conversation about this subject, it's another to have it part of public record.

That is the unfortunate circumstance we all find ourselves in. So much of what is happening with the mentally ill, generally, is not OK. Many are still prevented from calling out the injustices and pushing the hard truth forward. This has truly rattled me, but cannot stop me from moving forward. I don't blame anyone for having to protect themselves; I just wish it wasn't necessary. Hopefully, the future will be brighter for the fact that they spoke up at all.

I have met up with a few of our interviewees to get a quick idea of how they are doing from the time of their interview to the time we are wrapping up this book in August, 2015.

Christina, my daughter, who was the catalyst in all of this, had three interviews. We spoke with her approximately sixteen months ago, and a lot has changed in her life since then. Here's how she is doing.

> "It's been sixteen months since I last checked in with you guys. At that time I was cleaning boats… It didn't end so well.

That summer I had a completely manic episode which lead to another year of recovery. It's been a long road of fixing medication. I got put back on my old medication, which had originally worked for two years. My new medication didn't seem to work as effectively, so I was put back on my old dose and I started stabilizing. I started doing well. Things started to get better. I lost some weight. Obviously, it's still not perfect; some days I do resonate a little high, and always with that there does seem to come a bit of a low. So I do increase my medication a little on days I'm feeling rough, which seems to snap me back into myself by the next morning.

"Lots of good things are happening now that I am stabling out, even when I'm overwhelmed or am just having a bad day. For the most part, I'm living and functioning like a normal human being, which is amazing. I actually just moved out of my Mom's house, which is a big step for me: not having my Mom there to help me so much, and not having her around all the time. It's challenging, but I think it was what was best for us. I knew I was ready. I've also got a new job to support the fact I am living on my own. I am trying to apply for aid through disability to help keep me afloat. I'm finally feeling like myself. It's been almost three years since I felt like Christina. I feel really good. I look forward to getting up each morning, which hasn't been happening for the past few years."

Jacquie was originally interviewed as one of my first guests for this effort. She has a unique and an important story, not only because she is a social worker, but also as the Mother of a young man who has struggled with mental health and addiction issues for his whole life. Jacquie had this to say.

> "Since the last time I talked to you, which was just over a year ago, a lot has happened, which comes with the ebbs and flows of mental health issues. My son has had some successes and failures. One success is that he's entered rehab for the first time in ten years and is coming off methamphetamine for a lengthy period of time. He still struggles with his impulsivity, his mental health issues, making really poor choices, and struggling with coming to the point where he can be more independent as a young person.
>
> "For myself, it is a family matter and it does affect all of us. I have a history of post-traumatic stress which has a lot to do with what my son has gone through, and I'm having to take a break now and do some trauma treatment. The hard part about that is that I love my child, but his own inability to control himself is traumatic itself. So I'm working on that, but it's hard to find supports, and ones that are not private. It is very costly, but I'm working on it and I'm very optimistic. There definitely needs to be more psychiatrists available to accommodate people who need these supports, regardless of their financial situation.

Danica Brown is the membership manager for Workman Arts, an organization that employs the mentally ill through art opportunities. We originally interviewed Danica a year ago, and we met up with her recently to see how she was. Here is what she had to say.

"At Workman Arts we have expanded our scaling program, developing modes and best practices to make sure we can reach other cities, provinces, and hopefully other countries. Our executive director and founder, Lisa Brown, has received the Order of Canada this year, along with Catherine Zahn, the CEO of CAMH (Canadian Association for Mental Health).

"*Rendezvous with Madness* Film Festival has a brand new programmer, Mr. Jeff Paverr, who's amazing and really on top of his game. He's brought a lot of amazing films to the board already, so stay tuned and stay pinned on the website for more information for this year's festival and of course, our annual programming.

"As for me, I've started a band, Mama Motown and Her Bad Decisions—a complete ode to Motown music in all of its glory. You can follow us on the Facebook site, Mama Motown, on Instagram @MamaMotownBrown, and on Twitter @MamaMotown for any of our gigs, pictures or videos. We've had a lot of gigs at the Toronto Islands this summer—we've played at the Toronto Island Marina, the Toronto Island Sailing Club, and the Queen's City Yacht Club. We're also headed to Port Perry in September, and that's just the beginning.

"As for boat life, I am into my third year of living on a boat all year round, and it's still awesome. Plus I get to meet some awesome people. I also got to sing on the CAMH grounds in Toronto for the Pam Am Torch Relay this year as the torch was being run in, and again as the torch was being run out. If

> you follow CAMH News, there's a little clip of me doing Proud Mary next to Catherine Zahn, CEO of CAMH, the one who ran the torch."

Julie, the mother of Sophie, checked in a year after her interview. After years of no support, they have finally received some help. Here's what she had to say.

> "So it's been a year since we spoke, and in the last year we have tapped into many resources. The McMaster Children's Hospital has been our greatest resource, and we have attended as a family a twenty-week Dialectal Behaviour Therapy (DBT) training session, which is a take on cognitive behaviour therapy created especially for those with borderline personality disorder and is extremely effective with people with that diagnosis.

> "After the course, Sophie has continued to see a therapist one-on-one, every week, with the same program and she's made some progress. However, this year she's gone from thirteen to fourteen, and so we've treated some problems and had new problems we've had to adjust for. We are still struggling, but Ian and I are definitely better equipped to handle the struggles that come our way because we've been in that training session.

> "As of this morning, we were in with the one-on-one therapist, who wants to switch things up with Sophie and is now going to include me so that Sophie and I can work on our relationship. At the moment it's really strained, and

conversation is just not happening in any sort of effective way.

"Although we are still struggling, we have a great deal of help, and just having people to talk to, makes things just a little bit easier. When things get explosive or out of hand, I've got a couple of different numbers I can call and get some advice, which is really helpful. Currently, we have not received a diagnosis. It's a mood disorder, not otherwise specified, and I don't think we will see any sort of diagnosis until she's eighteen or nineteen."

We are at the closing stages of this project, and already I know that I have to move forward. I have more to do. The whole point of this project was to ensure that parents received some good, worthwhile information from people out there dealing with or affected by mental illness. I really wanted parents specifically to have the opportunity to hear other people's stories; to hear other people's triumphs, and other people's challenges. I didn't want them to feel by themselves. I really wanted them to feel like they had a community out there that might understand what they're going through.

In putting this effort together I now have more information to share. Our next effort will have information on some alternative therapies, as well as more conversations surrounding children and mental health.

I, like most parents, like to think the impossible is possible; that Christina will no longer need to spend so much of her day managing her meds, her moods, and her incessant and omnipresent anxiety.

What if there was a magic therapy? A special cocktail of something totally natural that would even-off her brain so she wouldn't go through such drastic states? What if I could wake up one morning without worrying about Christina's mood management? What would it be like to tell people she's working at a full-time, high-end job in Toronto instead of attending an outpatient day program at our local hospital? What would it be like to fall asleep without having a gloomy thought that Christina is about to fall off the rails? What if she could do the things normal young people can do? Travel the world, or even have her own children? That is why I need to do another instalment of Different from the Other Kids.

I have spoken to people that I want to interview that have had great success in treating mental illness by natural means. I have a couple of people I want to interview, who think about mental illness differently and I think are worth hearing out. Treatment by natural means is possible for some. For the rest, how about if we learn to accept and even surrender to these imperfections of the brain? What if we could just accept the person for who they are, and celebrate what they CAN do? Let's keep concentrating on giving parents real information and real life accounts of other families that struggle.

I am excited to go forward and make this to happen. We've got this down, and my project manager, my nephew Jesse Bickerton, has been exceptional in getting us organized. I'm hoping to get this effort out to you within a twelve month period, to keep it relevant and to keep it fresh.

So stay tuned (or should I say, stay iTuned!)

Listen to the Different From the Other Kids Podcast

If you like to listen as well as read, all the interviews that this book is based on are available on iTunes, as episodes of Angela's podcast of the same name: *Different from the Other Kids*.

> http://www.dftok.com/podcast-info

Reader Resources

Remember!

Angela and her guests have put together a collection of resources to help parents of challenging children. It includes nutrition and exercise advice, checklists and other useful tips and information.

You can get a copy by visiting

http://www.dftok.com/bonus-page

If you'd like to contact Angela directly, you can email her at
team@dftok.com

www.ingramcontent.com/pod-product-compliance
Lightning Source LLC
Chambersburg PA
CBHW062141280426
43673CB00072B/115